RISE
OF THE
READER

STRATEGIES FOR MASTERING YOUR READING
HABITS AND APPLYING WHAT YOU LEARN

RISE
OF THE
READER

Bonus: 100+ Healthy, Wealthy, and
Happy Habits You Can Start Implementing Today

NICK HUTCHISON

Contact information for The Reading Revolution Publishing – nick@implementingbooks.com

ISBN: 979-8-9880909-0-8 (paperback)
ISBN: 979-8-9880909-1-5 (ebook)
ISBN: 979-8-9880909-2-2 (hardcover)
ISBN: 979-8-9880909-3-9 (audiobook)

Library of Congress Control Number: 2023911792

Printed in Taunton, MA, U.S.A.

Ordering Information:
Special discounts are available on quantity purchases by corporations, associations, and others. For details, contact nick@implementingbooks.com or go to www.riseofthereaderbook.com

Publisher's Cataloging-in-Publication Data

Names: Hutchison, Nicholas Thomas, 1993- .
Title: Rise of the reader : strategies for mastering your reading habits / Nick Hutchison.
Description: Taunton, MA : The Reading Revolution, 2023. | Includes index and bibliographic references.
Identifiers: LCCN 2023911792 | ISBN 9798988090922 (hardback) | ISBN 9798988090908 (pbk) |
    ISBN 9798988090915 (ebook) | ISBN 9798988090939 (audio)
Subjects: LCSH: Reading (Adult education). | Reading comprehension. | Self-help techniques. |
    BISAC: LANGUAGE ARTS & DISCIPLINES / Reading Skills. | SELF-HELP / Personal Growth /
    General.
Classification: LCC BF456.2 H88 2023 | DDC 158.1 H--dc23
LC record available at https://lccn.loc.gov/2023911792

"Those who keep learning will keep *rising* in life."[1] – Charlie Munger

To Mom and Dad,

This book is dedicated to you both. Throughout my life, you have always encouraged me to pursue my dreams and cheered me on at every step of the way. Your belief in me, your endless patience, and your unconditional love have been incredible. You've taught me the value of perseverance, the beauty of ambition, and the importance of staying true to myself. I am eternally grateful for the countless sacrifices you've made and the boundless encouragement you've offered.

Without your constant presence in my life, I would not be the person I am today.

This book is a testament to the power of love and the strength of a supportive family. Thank you both for being my biggest champions and for always believing in me. I dedicate this work to you both, with all my heart.

#familyfirst

Nick

Guiding Principles

Reality is negotiable. Reality is limitless.

The right book at the right time can change your life.

Table of Contents

Reading Tips

15 Minutes

Studies show that less than 50% of adults have finished a book in the last year.[2] Use the following advice to ensure that you don't find yourself in that category. Instead of trying to "find" time to read, you can simply replace low-impact activities with reading personal development books. A little less Netflix or Instagram and a little more self-development never hurt anyone. Check out this math:

- 15 minutes of reading = roughly 10 pages (for beginners)
- 10 pages in the morning + 10 pages in the evening = 20 pages /day
- 20 pages/day * 5 weekdays = 100 pages/week
- 100 pages/week * 52 weeks = 5,200 pages/year
- 5,200 pages/year ÷ 250 pages/book = **OVER 20 BOOKS**

By replacing 15 minutes of your morning Instagram scrolling and the first 15 minutes of your evening Netflix session with reading, you can improve 20 different areas of your life within the next year.

Plus, the benefits from watching Netflix or scrolling on Instagram (short dopamine hits) can fade the moment you stop them, whereas the benefits from reading (genuine fulfillment) can last a lifetime. Looking back, I can't even remember the names of the main characters from shows I watched six months ago. Sad, but true!

Set an Intention

Before diving into a personal development book, I take a moment to define my intention. What am I hoping to gain from this book? What specific outcome do I want it to help me achieve?

The greater the personal and emotional investment you have in your intention, the more likely you are to discover transformative insights within the book that can lead to real change in your life.

I suggest jotting down your intention on the inside cover of a physical book or on a sticky note attached to the back of your e-book/audio device. Reviewing your intention every time you begin reading will keep your mind attuned to the information most relevant to your desired outcome, empowering you to take practical steps toward achieving your goal.

Since my early days of reading, I've made it a habit to sign and date the inside cover of each book I start as well. It's a personal tradition I enjoy, and looking back at some of the first books I read and seeing my name and the date brings a warm sense of nostalgia. Adding a personal touch to lending books, I also invite friends to sign their names when borrowing one of my books, creating a sense of connection.

It's surprising how often I encounter a blank stare when I ask someone about their current read and the reason they're reading it. It's important to know your motivation for reading a book, as it serves as a compass for the direction of your personal growth. Understanding why you're reading something allows you to actively engage with the material, reflect on its relevance to your life, and ultimately, make meaningful connections that can create growth and development.

You need to know why you're reading a book.

Take a few minutes to think about and define your intention for reading THIS BOOK. Are you looking to get more out of the other books you're reading? Are you trying to take better notes? Improve retention? Are you looking to become healthier, wealthier, or happier?

An example might be, "My intention for reading this book is to find and implement at least three note-taking strategies by the end of next week. I want to learn how to retain more from the books I am reading so that I can implement their lessons and live up to my potential in life. I am done living a life of mediocrity. I owe it to my family, my friends, and myself to be healthier, wealthier, and happier."

Review your intention each time you open this book and you'll be amazed with the results.

Our brains have a natural highlighter called the Reticular Activating System (RAS) that helps us filter out the irrelevant or unimportant inputs to our brain and highlights the important ones. By defining our intention for each book and reviewing it constantly, we are telling our conscious self *and* our subconscious self what information to highlight and retain.

Rising Readers leverage the power of intention by transforming reading from a form of entertainment to a form of education. Average readers struggle from intention deficit disorder, but thankfully, you now know one of the greatest strategies for getting more from what you read. **The stronger your intention, the more you will retain and implement from the books you're reading.**

Really try to feel your intention and create as much top-of-mind emotion as you can when referring back to it.

Read with Friends

Do you have anyone in your network who could also benefit from reading this book?

I believe we are the average of the five people we spend the most time with. **One of the best ways to raise the average of your group is to grow together.** By purchasing a copy of this book for a few of your friends and holding each other accountable to reading it, you can all take advantage of what you're learning. Plus, one of the fun things about personal development books is that each person will have a different set of takeaways and a different perspective on how to apply what they're learning. This additional perspective can be beneficial to your own reading experience as well.

If you're interested in layering in some additional accountability, take a quick flip through Chapter 8, Success Buddies. Throughout that chapter, I teach you how to create a high-performance accountability group that gets the most out of books like this one. If that sounds too intense for you and you would rather begin with a smaller commitment, I recommend forming a small informal book club with your friends in a group chat. This way you can just send your favorite lessons to the group and start to formulate some conversation that way.

Plus, what better way to grow closer to your best friends and family than by gifting them a copy of something that can dramatically change their lives for the better. I won't let you down!

Read with the Audiobook

Have you ever tried reading a book while simultaneously following along with the audiobook?

It might sound a little strange, but it's one of my favorite reading tips for keeping yourself on pace and eliminating distractions. Simply purchase the audiobook and play it in the background as you're reading.

This dynamic approach to reading can significantly enhance your comprehension and engagement with the material. By pairing the written text with the spoken words, you create a multi-sensory experience that taps into both visual and auditory processing. This can be particularly beneficial for complex or dense content, as the audiobook can help clarify challenging passages or unfamiliar terms, while the act of reading keeps your focus sharp. Give it a shot and discover how this harmonious combination of reading and listening can elevate your reading adventure to a whole new level.

PART I:
Introduction to Personal Development

1. What's All the Hype?

I vividly remember driving to my local Barnes & Noble bookstore for the first time.

A few weeks earlier, I'd discovered that there was a massive gap between the person I was—insecure and self-centered—and the person I wanted to be—secure and focused on serving others. That realization initially frightened me, but I am grateful that I chose to confront the discomfort head-on instead of avoiding it. A veil was lifted, and I felt fully awake for the first time.

It was 2015, and I had just secured a summer sales internship with a small software firm, and with just a year remaining before graduation, I was eager to gain some work experience before I graduated and was forced into a nine-to-five lifestyle.

My new boss Kyle became a mentor. He was an avid podcast listener and would put on personal development and business podcasts whenever we had long car rides together.

He explained to me that while he enjoyed listening to music, he realized that replaying a song for the 300th time wasn't going to get him closer to his dream life. He understood that, on the other hand, the right personal development podcast might.

Growing up, I wasn't receptive to this kind of educational content. After observing the positive impact these shows were having on Kyle, I decided to incorporate them into my daily commute routine. Up until that point, I held a belief that business podcasts were solely meant for dull and boring businesspeople. Yet, Kyle was a personable guy who loved to party and have a good time. I soon realized that investing in personal growth was a predictor for success and should be discussed confidently.

Those first couple of weeks were eye-opening to me. I tried many different podcast formats, but I found the most value in those where the host interviewed successful people and talked with them about what they had done to become successful. The advice was always very practical and so, in no time at all, I had a laundry list of subjects that I wanted to learn more about.

This is where my initial interest in personal development books came from. So many of these podcasters and their guests were recommending titles, and I began to hear some of the same ones over and over. These people made it seem like I was missing out on the world's best kept secrets by choosing not to read.

In one podcast, the guest said that successful people often condense decades of their life experience into mere days by writing books. As readers, we can consume that information quickly and use it to navigate future obstacles, saving us a boatload of time and headaches. Personal experience is a great teacher, but another person's experience can be even better because you can learn the lesson without feeling the pain.

Time to hit the bookstore and find out what the hype was all about! Little did I know that the books I was about to purchase would dramatically change my life.

My First Books

Armed with the shopping list I'd compiled from the podcasts I'd listened to, I cautiously entered Barnes & Noble. This first trip took place during my internship lunch hour, so I didn't have too much time to shop around before I had to return to the office.

I remember being in awe of how many personal development books were available. So. Many. Options. I was equally overwhelmed and excited at the same time. As I browsed the endless shelves, there seemed to be a book for just about every problem in my life.

Consulting my list, I grabbed copies of *Rich Dad Poor Dad* and *Cashflow Quadrant* by Robert T. Kiyosaki and Sharon Lechter; *The Art of War* by Sun Tzu; *The Richest Man in Babylon* by George S. Clayson; and *The 7 Habits of Highly Effective People* by Stephen R. Covey. I was delighted to find everything I was looking for, and I even grabbed a handful of other titles that caught my attention on the way to the cashier.

As I went to pay, I experienced a moment of uncertainty as I thought about my bank account. Should a college student without much money be spending what little he has on books? At around $20 per book, I was about to spend almost $200. Thankfully, I remembered another lesson I had learned during one of my podcast sessions:

The best investment you can make is in yourself. The most cost-effective investment in yourself is not a formal education, a week-long retreat, or an online course…it's a book. Why? Books only cost $20 and take just a few hours to consume, yet they hold the same power to change your life as any of those other resources. The potential return on investment (ROI) is insane!

At the checkout, I signed up for a store membership card. I knew that to really shift my identity from a non-reader to a reader, I had to commit. Carrying the membership card around in my wallet seemed like something a reader would do. Plus, I got a good discount for signing up, which made me feel better. By simply buying a few books, I could already feel my potential starting to grow. It was as if instantly, a switch had been flipped, and I was now on a very different path in life.

Since my responsibilities during that internship weren't particularly time-consuming, I spent a fair amount of that afternoon and the rest of that summer reading those books. My reading speed was slow, and I wasn't sure how to take effective notes or implement what I was learning, but I was hooked. I began with *Rich Dad Poor Dad*—I still have that copy today.

I am so grateful that I chose to read it first. *Rich Dad Poor Dad* was actionable, easy to understand, educational, and short enough for a new reader like me to get through in a few days. If I had started with a different book, I might have disliked it, given up, and shelved the rest of the books I'd purchased. Unfortunately, that happens to a lot of new readers.

A book is not valuable to a reader unless it gives them something to implement, an action that will change their lives for the better. Yet the truth is, we as readers get to choose what to implement and for most readers, they choose to implement nothing. I know many people who have read *Rich Dad Poor Dad* and found it useless. For me, it changed *everything*.

Being a business student who didn't yet know much about money, something amazing happened after reading these initial books, most of which were about personal finance and investing. In a matter of weeks, I went from someone who withdrew from conversations about money to someone who frequently led them. I went from someone who shied away from setting a post-graduation earnings goal to someone who was looking at multiple six-figure opportunities.

If that could happen after reading just a few books, I began thinking about other areas of my life to which I could apply this new superpower. This obvious solution to every problem I was facing was hiding in plain sight—and for only $20 a pop. Was I really on track to level up in every area of my life?

Growing Up

I had the best childhood. My parents worked hard to give my younger brothers and me that 'white picket fence' type family experience. I had friends in the neighborhood, trees to climb, and I played a lot of sports. I was always healthy and ate well, I received tons of love from my parents, and we had plenty of presents under the Christmas tree every year. Outside of some social anxiety, I was always very happy.

Not much changed as I got a bit older. I played football and was the captain of our high school wrestling team. Having three younger brothers, all close in age, I developed a love for competition that I still hold today. I could find a way to turn just about anything, physical or intellectual, into a competition. The upside was that I gained confidence in certain areas of my life, but the downside was that my confidence eventually developed into an ego and sense of entitlement. I wasn't always the most fun to be around and I spent a lot of time focusing on myself, sometimes at the expense of others.

The one area where I lacked confidence was in my ability to communicate in front of new people. When I was in a small group of friends that I felt comfortable with, I thrived when all eyes were on me—it felt great. However, the moment I had to present in front of the class or go outside of my comfort zone, anxiety would punch me in the face. You know that feeling? Heart thumping and a pit in your stomach? I didn't understand the benefits of embracing discomfort back then, which meant that I did anything I could to avoid those public-speaking situations.

I suppose this form of social anxiety is why I was never a reader growing up. Most class presentations happened in the reading-intensive classes like English, Spanish, or history. I remember being above average in critical thinking and private test-taking subjects like math, but way below average in oral communication and presentation-based subjects like the ones mentioned above.

Unfortunately, the public education system and classroom dynamics I grew up in taught students to avoid failure at all costs. The thought of stuttering or misreading something in front of the entire class and having everyone laugh terrified me.

There were times where I would pretend to be sick on presentation days so that my parents would let me stay home. That way, I could work with teachers one-on-one after school instead of speaking in front of my peers. I even used to get up and head to the bathroom before it was my turn to read out loud in English class. My social anxiety was crippling, but because I cared way too much about what people thought of me, I did a great job at hiding it.

That was my reality back then, and I put in a lot of hard work over the years to change it. **I know now that failure leads to progress, and it should not be discouraged. In fact, I believe that embracing failure is one of the first building blocks for success.**

Since I disliked school and spent a lot of time playing sports, I was always looking for shortcuts. I would read book summaries online instead of the actual books and rely on other students to help me get by. That same behavior followed me into college. I didn't realize it then, but I had some major problems to fix. On one hand, I was self-centered and full of ego. On the other, I was doing anything I could to navigate my social anxiety, causing me to live with a lot of fear.

Since my mom worked in retail management and my dad in athletic footwear sales, I decided that the business world was where I belonged. I was accepted into the University of New Hampshire and took entry-level business classes during my first semester. My early professors encouraged me to find a summer internship where I could explore the different areas of business and discover something that I liked. Throughout my years at school, I secured two placements that totally changed my life.

The first was in a company that helped college students run their own house painting businesses during the summer. Focused on the earning potential, I totally missed the fact that I would have to generate my own sales by knocking on doors every weekend and then hire college students to complete the jobs I sold.

I could fill this whole book with the mistakes I made during that first summer. However, those same mistakes resulted in me facing some of my social anxiety—and my ego.

Through my experiences door-to-door selling, I was starting to learn how to communicate more effectively. I was constantly humbled by the rejection. The biggest lesson of all? **You can become comfortable with anything.** Remember those social anxiety nerves that caused me to stay home from school? They were showing up less frequently. All it took was a bit of courage and some basic repetition.

In fact, out of every aspect of the job, which included marketing, selling, operations, management, and finance, I found the most enjoyment in selling. After two full summers of running a house painting business, I realized that I needed to get more sales experience and improve my communication skills in order to secure a great job after graduation. I enrolled in some public-speaking classes and spent my final summer at the software internship I mentioned above, where I discovered my passion for books.

My social anxiety from high school had created certain barriers to my learning. Thankfully, I was still open enough to take my boss Kyle's suggestions and begin exploring podcasts. Having a fixed mindset where you believe that you're already the best and that there is nothing out there to learn is a very dangerous place to be.

Did I come out of the womb reading books? No. Not even close. For years, I was able to read but actively chose not to. I was living under my potential. Now, I embrace the universal truth that we are all capable of becoming more and designing our dream life.

The ability to read these books and apply their teachings is one of the most underutilized skills we have today.

Reading Time

I can't even imagine what my life would be like if I hadn't started reading personal development books. I can guarantee, though, that it wouldn't be nearly as fulfilling. I am now in my late 20s and have read hundreds of books. The math is mind-boggling to me:

- 400+ books
- Average of 250 pages/book
- 400+ books * 250 pages = 100,000+ pages

If you had tapped me on the shoulder in high school and told me that I was going to read and digest 100,000 pages of information before I was 30, I would have called you crazy.

When I started my reading journey, I was a very slow reader. We will discuss reading speed later, but for now, know that reading can be broken down into a set of individual skills. Each of these skills can be improved with time, repetition, and better strategies. For the sake of simplicity, let's say that I read at an average of .67 pages (two thirds of a page) per minute:

- 100,000 pages = 150,000 minutes
- 150,000 minutes / 60 minutes = 2,500 hours of reading

Is that a lot of time? I am not sure. It's not the 10,000 hours that Malcolm Gladwell talks about in his blockbuster book *Outliers*, but I am sure when you include the time I have spent implementing everything I have read, I would be close to 10,000 hours. Take that, Malcolm!

My life has been completely transformed, and I owe just about everything I have now to those 2,500 hours of reading. I am healthier, wealthier, and happier than I have ever been, and I am continuing to make more progress.

For years now, I have worked in the book industry and my businesses have given me access to tens of thousands of non-fiction readers on a weekly basis. I receive all sorts of questions, and I am going to address dozens of the most common ones throughout this book: How do I choose the right book? How should I take notes? How can I apply what I'm learning?

My promise to you is that by the time you're done reading the first half of this book, you'll have the strategies and framework to effectively retain and implement more from the books you read. The right book at the right time can change your life...especially if you implement what they teach you effectively.

The second half will introduce over 100 habits that I've implemented in my own life from the books I've read. I'll take you through my experiences of implementing them—the good, the bad, and the ugly—and they will, in turn, be motivators for you too.

I wrote this book because I wish I'd had access to this information when I was starting my reading journey back in 2015. It took hundreds of books and countless failed attempts at implementing them before I came up with the strategies and best practices that I share with you here.

Do you have to read 400+ books to design your dream life? Absolutely not. I have condensed many of my favorite life lessons from the books I've read into this one so that you can accelerate your journey. Consider this book a cheat code, giving you the tools to navigate the world of personal development with ease.

This book is not designed to entertain you; this book is designed to educate you.

Nowadays, I am focused on helping as many people as possible bridge the gap between who they are today and who they can become. I see books as the vehicle to bridge that gap because that is how I was able to do it.

Back in 2018, I started sharing the books that I was reading on social media and writing short book reviews. Eventually, my following grew to a point where authors were reaching out and asking if they could pay me to review their books. Get paid to read? That sounded like a dream. Fast forward a few years and my business, BookThinkers, is helping hundreds of authors connect with more readers and helping thousands of readers find the right authors to guide and inform them. This work makes me very happy.

This is my world, and I can't wait to walk you through it.

Living Under Your Potential

Early in my reading journey, someone recommended *The Top Five Regrets of the Dying* by Bronnie Ware to me. Reading that book changed my perspective on life and death.

As an end-of-life caretaker, Bronnie spent a lot of time with the dying. She found that most people on their deathbed wish they'd had the courage to live a life true to themselves, not the life others expected of them. It was heartbreaking to read about these people who had finally achieved a sense of clarity about what truly mattered to them but couldn't act on it because they were near the end of their life. They were prisoners of their own regret.

Regret is poison. Living below your potential will poison you. As human beings, we have a finite amount of time here—you don't want to be on your deathbed wishing you had done more with your life.

There are two deathbed visualizations that really drive this point home for me. I encourage you to spend a few minutes reflecting on each of them now:

Deathbed Visualization #1

Picture yourself at Heaven's Gate, ready to look back on your life and receive judgment. As you're standing there, you look to your right and see other versions of yourself. Those versions of you talk about a life of no regrets. They speak of pursuing their passions relentlessly, facing each opportunity with unwavering faith. They talk about striving to be the best version of themselves for their family and friends. In life, they were truly healthy, wealthy, and happy. Then they turn to you and ask, "How about you? Did you take advantage of this once-in-a-lifetime opportunity and explore all of what life has to offer?"

Given your current life trajectory, how would you answer? Let it sink in.

At any given moment, we have an infinite number of choices in front of us, which means there are infinite future versions of ourselves out there. Some decisions will get us closer to happiness and fulfillment whereas others won't. The beautiful (and scary) thing is that we are in control of those choices.

Deathbed Visualization #2

Picture yourself on your deathbed, alone, unable to get up and realize your unfulfilled dreams. An angel appears and calmly asks, "How much would you be willing to spend to magically go back in time to (*insert the year you're reading this*) and experience a few days with your family and friends?"

Really think about it for a moment. I bet you'd be willing to spend anything, right? You'd go back in time and live life to the fullest, taking nothing for granted, especially your time. The sad part is that no amount of money will allow you to travel back in time, regain mobility, and spend time with your loved ones.

We all admire the wealth that Warren Buffett has accumulated, but I'll bet that none of us would trade places with him. At the time of this writing, Warren is 92 years old. Our youth, whether we're 18 or 80, is everything. We can't buy back time.

Now, snap back to reality and experience the present moment with old eyes.

What is stopping you from living up to your full potential right now? Fear of judgment? Fear of failure? The author Steven Pressfield calls the forces that hold us back "resistance."

The strangest part about the resistance we face is that it comes from within. We create our own resistance. The fears that push us to live under our potential are nothing more than figments of our own imagination. They are not forced upon us, and they don't exist when we are gone.

Don't fall prey to the idea that you are going to live forever.

According to the CDC, the average lifespan for someone living in the US is 77.[3] That means that by 38.5, you're already halfway there. Focus on this and let the magic of mortality guide your actions.

The beautiful thing is that this heightened awareness of your own mortality also creates vulnerability, reflection, and an openness to learn.

Do not ignore the moments of your life that offer you the opportunity to learn the most.

This book is one of those moments.

The good news is that if you are reading this, you're already on the way to changing your life. Most people buy books like this and then ignore them. Stick with it, because as this book progresses, so does its value.

The world needs more thinkers.

2. Lifestyle Design

I was originally introduced to the concept of Lifestyle Design in *The 4-Hour Workweek*, written by one of my favorite authors, Tim Ferriss.

Reading his book and implementing what I learned completely changed my life. The following is one of my favorite quotes from the book:

> "Gold is getting old. The New Rich (NR) are those who abandon the deferred-life plan and create luxury lifestyles in the present using the currency of the New Rich: time and mobility. This is an art and a science we will refer to as Lifestyle Design (LD)."[4]

Tim wrote about his adventures all over the world and the freedom to do it all without worrying about money, while only working a few hours per week. At first, I thought Tim was exaggerating—and a little unhinged. That's not how the world works...right?

Now, I strongly believe that we should be able to live however we want to and bend reality to meet our individual needs.

I had been searching for a way to stay focused on designing my life but kept slipping back into my old thought patterns and bad habits.

Then, I found out why.

Reality Is Negotiable

Have you ever heard of neuro-linguistic programming (NLP)?[5]

The idea is that we humans have thousands of thoughts per day. Research shows that as many as 90% of these thoughts are the same every day. Unfortunately, for a lot of people, these are overwhelmingly negative and fear-based, although most are unconscious. NLP is a practice where we try to consciously detect and modify these limiting beliefs so that they support the life we are designing, not undermine it.

If you're dreaming of changing the world, going against the grain, or at least living a life that fulfills you, you must start by rewiring your brain.

Up until recently, scientists thought our brains were fixed and couldn't be changed much once we became adults. Fortunately, we have come to realize that the human brain is malleable, meaning it can adapt. These brain changes can happen in a few different ways, but what we have the most control over is slow and steady change.

This concept becomes clear when you think about your default neural pathways, the connections that form between the neurons in your brain. Let's say that each time you're presented with a challenge at work, you start thinking about the consequences if you fail, which causes your brain to panic. This is commonly referred to as a flight response. What would happen if instead of focusing on failure, you focused on a successful outcome to each challenge? You envision yourself growing, learning new skills, getting a pat on the back, and getting a raise. Well, over time, you'd start to default to that pathway instead, which is commonly referred to as a fight response.

What default responses exist in your life today that you could rewire and update for better health, wealth, and happiness? This process happens slowly and through repetition, but over time, small adaptations can result in big changes to your brain.

One of the first ways I implemented this was by placing little positive cues in my environment. Every time they caught my attention, they changed the way my unconscious brain was thinking. I started identifying more with who I wanted to be than with who society wanted me to be.

Play Bigger Triggers

I call these little positive environmental cues "Play Bigger Triggers" (PBTs), which I first heard from a mentor and friend of mine, Evan Carmichael, whose book *Built to Serve* helped me define and articulate my purpose in life. PBTs are one of the most powerful tools I am aware of for rewiring your brain.

When I first heard of the concept, I started writing positive quotes on sticky notes and leaving them on my bathroom mirror and in my workspace. Day after day, whenever I felt unmotivated or fearful, I would read the sticky notes, which gradually started to rewire my brain to default to a more positive and motivated state.

After loving the results, I invested in some motivational artwork for the walls of my office and a bunch of slogan T-shirts with messages like, "Think Big." I even updated my online passwords to contain abbreviated versions of my favorite motivational quotes.

If you want to know how much I believe in this concept, look no further than my tattoos:

Play Bigger Trigger Tattoo Example #1

When I started my reading journey, it was very clear to me that the most successful people focused on what they had in life, whereas unsuccessful people focused only on what they lacked. Focusing on what you have is called gratitude.

I read that many successful people journal daily about what they are grateful for, so I started to do the same. Every morning, I would write down at least three things I was grateful for. Funny enough, as a result, I naturally started to think about things I was thankful for throughout the day.

Instead of seeing a fancy car on the highway and thinking, "Wow, I wish I had that car," I would think, "Wow, I am so happy to have a car, knowing that many people aren't as fortunate." This left me feeling more positive, more of the time. I decided to get the numbers 1) 2) 3) tattooed on my left wrist so that dozens of times per day, every day, whether consciously or unconsciously, I see the tattoo and make sure my default pathway is gratitude.

Imagine you woke up tomorrow and everything you never expressed gratitude for disappeared. Start now!

Play Bigger Trigger Tattoo Example #2

On my right wrist, I have the phrase "Reality is Negotiable" tattooed. I discovered this phrase in *The 4-Hour Workweek*. Society can be very persistent, and I knew that each time I was presented with the pressure to conform to society's expectations, I would need a reminder that Lifestyle Design is what I truly want. I want time and mobility, not a traditional nine-to-five and a ton of bad debt.

I have consulted this tattoo thousands of times consciously and tens of thousands of times unconsciously over the last five years or so. Each time, I am reminded of my core values and that I can bend reality to my will. You can't beat me, society!

Play Bigger Trigger Tattoo Example #3

Memento mori is a Latin phrase that translates literally to "Remember you must die."[6] At first glance, this seems dark and chilling. As we discussed in Chapter 1, too many of us overestimate the amount of time we have on this beautiful planet, and as a result, we procrastinate and constantly put our dreams off until tomorrow. Then at the end of our lives, we wind up regretting the time we wasted on meaningless activities.

By constantly reminding ourselves we have a limited amount of time to chase our dreams, we will prioritize our time more efficiently and take less of it for granted. As a daily reminder, I had *Memento mori* tattooed on my chest, right above my heart. Whenever I am feeling lazy or unproductive, I simply look in the mirror and focus on my heart beating below the tattoo—my vitality. It won't beat forever. We are mortal.

Moral of the story? Get positive tattoos!

I am partly kidding, but the principle of positive, forward-thinking NLP stays the same. Positive cues in your environment will help you default to who you want to be, not who society wants you to be. For me, any environmental cue that supports me is a PBT.

Recently, I was chatting with the legendary author, Steven Pressfield, about this subject. He told me he keeps a little replica cannon on his desk and whenever he feels resistance, he aims the cannon at himself so that it can fire inspiration in his direction.

Does that sound funny to you? Not to me. I know it works. I bought a cannon for my desk as well. Trust me, you can rewire your brain to default to whatever you want to have, and you can use PBTs to keep you in that headspace.

How do you implement Play Bigger Triggers? Start by removing all the Play Smaller Triggers (PSTs) from your life—environmental cues that reinforce your limiting beliefs. An example of a PST might be a third-place trophy you keep on your bureau, a social media account you follow that constantly creates feelings of inferiority, or the messy workspace you've been tolerating for years. By removing these PSTs, you're already heading in the right direction.

Next, find opportunities to insert positive cues into your life. They can come in many forms, such as desk cannons, tattoos, sticky notes, motivational slogan T-shirts, online passwords, phone desktop wallpapers, artwork, books, souvenirs, jewelry, miscellaneous trinkets, people, and more. Yes, you are the average of the five people you spend the most time with and if those people are motivational, you will achieve more.

Once the PBTs are installed, your subconscious will start picking up on them without your conscious attention. To double down, consciously focus on them for a few moments whenever they catch your eye and reflect on who you're becoming.

Our minds are constantly looking for the path of least resistance and will always default to our comfort zone, so we need reminders of what we're looking to become if we want to disrupt these default tendencies.

Since I started listening to podcasts, reading personal development books, and installing PBTs that keep me focused on my dream life, I have made tremendous progress. Over the years, I have traveled, started businesses, and interviewed dozens of millionaires, billionaires, and world-changers. I have improved the relationships I have with everyone around me, overcome my social anxiety, and created a life focused on positively impacting as many people as I can. I eat well, get tons of sleep, and have eliminated all the negative stresses from my life...even the financial ones.

I am fulfilled, happy, and full of joy.

What Excites You?

What lifestyle energizes you? Whatever it is, I want you to know that Lifestyle Design is possible. Although society has created a framework that works for a lot of people, that doesn't mean it has to be right for you. You know what I'm talking about:

- Attend a four-year college and take on a ton of debt
- Land a job at a big company with a fancy business card
- Start a 401k retirement account in your early 20s
- Climb the "corporate ladder" and work more and more as you get older
- Buy expensive houses and cars while barely making enough money to pay the bills
- Retire at 65 (if you're lucky) so that you can start living your dream

If that's the lifestyle that fuels you, pursue it rigorously. If you're happy, no judgment.

If it isn't, follow a different path. Author MJ DeMarco calls that lifestyle, "Wealth in a wheelchair," and you don't have to settle for it. It took me a while to learn this, but you have more control over your life than you may think.

That lifestyle seems to lead to a lot of regret. Unhappy people encouraging (pressuring) you to conform and follow the same boring path they did? As I said earlier, I don't want any part in that. It doesn't make much sense to me.

But what should you do if you're unsure of what excites you? I am no expert on this subject but telling you how I was able to define my passion might help spark some ideas.

As you read in Chapter 1, I have never enjoyed the traditional classroom setting. Whether it was figuring out I could pass AP calculus in high school with a 0% homework average or realizing my college lectures could be attended from my dorm room by connecting the participation clicker to campus Wi-Fi, I wanted shortcuts.

The funny thing is that **although I disliked school, I loved education.** I was always teaching myself new things outside of the classroom. In the personal development community, there seems to be a consensus that **formal education will make you a living, but self-education will make you a fortune**. I always felt a strong resistance to formal education and a strong pull toward self-education. Clue number one.

Clue number two came from the resistance I felt to working in an office after graduating from college. Although my coworkers were pleasant people, I found the workplace distracting. I could always get better work done before everyone else got to the office or after everyone left—I was drawn toward working in a solo environment. On top of that, I found it limiting to have to get things approved by a boss instead of making decisions myself. In college, I ran my own business and made all the decisions at a moment's notice. Although it was scary at times, it was better than delegating the risk to someone else. Could entrepreneurship really be for me? This early? Clue number two became a daily question.

As I continued reading personal development books and listening to more podcasts, I came across the idea of practicing productive procrastination. What does that mean? It means that sometimes your side project, the thing you work on while you're procrastinating, is the real magic. It's the age-old question that gets tossed around: "What would you do if money was no object?"—except you're doing it anyway, even though you're not getting paid, and money is most likely still a problem. What was that side project for me? Reading personal development books, implementing what I was learning, and teaching it to others. Clue number three.

I took these clues into consideration, trusted them, and started creating a life that met these needs. No, the lifestyle I was designing did not meet society's expectations, but that was okay. I could combat criticism by simply saying, **"I am designing a life that fulfills me."**

We seek pleasure and avoid pain. Could it really be as simple as doing more of what excites us and less of what drains our energy? Yes. I do believe it is that simple. When you let that philosophy guide your decision-making, life starts to make a lot more sense.

Defining My Purpose

If you're living a life that fulfills you, is that the same thing as living with purpose?

The words *purpose* and *passion* have become popular over the years, but they have also become confusing. As my community started growing and I was asked to be interviewed on podcasts, I noticed I was being asked about my purpose more and more frequently. Although I was living a fulfilling life, I still had a hard time conveying my purpose or passion in a way that fully articulated how I felt. That remained true, at least until I read *Built to Serve*.

The author-mentor I mentioned earlier, Evan Carmichael, teaches the reader a framework that he calls Who, Why, How. By going through the exercises in his book and reflecting on what I was learning, I was able to define my purpose. I am now able to articulate my purpose in a clear and consistent manner:

- **Who**: Action. When I can take action and make progress in my health, wealth, or happiness, I am fulfilled. When I can help other people take action and make progress in their health, wealth, or happiness, I am also fulfilled. For me, action creates progress and progress equals happiness.

- **Why**: Only a few years ago, I was struggling with anxiety, ego, and insecurities. After reading and implementing some life-changing personal development books, I was able to change the trajectory of my life. I am now healthy, wealthy, and happy. I am motivated to help other people struggling with anxiety, ego, or insecurities to feel as fulfilled and as stable as I am.

- **How**: Right now, I am connecting people with books that can change their lives. This happens through social media, podcasting, and resources like this book. I am also enabling authors to connect their books with more readers by helping them optimize their social media, podcasting, and other resources. Same outcome.

How cool is that? Evan teaches us that our purpose comes from our pain, which makes a lot of sense to me—mine certainly did. So, avoid pain and seek pleasure, right? This clarity has been very useful for me. Having a consistent message allows you to focus more on your goals.

Now that you understand my love for personal development books and Lifestyle Design, it's time to become a Rising Reader.

3. Become a Rising Reader

The Rise of the Reader is the shift from reading as a form of entertainment to reading as a form of education and behavior change. Don't get me wrong...the two are not mutually exclusive. There are plenty of books that are both entertaining and educational. The point I am driving home here is that if your intention for reading is to improve your life, any other outcome is a failure.

Imagine three friends: Shaun, Luke, and Chandler. The three of them are looking to improve their overall happiness and decide to read this book over the next few weeks. Unfortunately, as the weeks go by, Shaun fails to schedule reading time and defaults to watching Netflix and playing video games. Luke reads the book but fails to take notes and review his original intention for reading the book and therefore, doesn't implement anything useful into his life. Chandler, on the other hand, sets a strong intention for the book, takes amazing notes, and adds his biggest happiness takeaways into his habit tracker so that he can start implementing them.

The outcome? Chandler is happier, whereas for Shaun and Luke, nothing changes. They stay stuck in the same place. In this scenario, even though Luke spent five or six hours reading this book, he failed to read effectively and act on what he learned, and because of that, there was no difference between his reading and Shaun's Netflix and video games.

Reading a great book is no different than watching Netflix or playing video games when you fail to use it to positively change your life. In that scenario, the book becomes a form of entertainment, not education.

No books + no implementation = no change

Books + no implementation = no change

Books + implementation = change

Knowing these books can change your life and choosing not to implement what you're learning is like knowing you're guaranteed to win the lottery but choosing not to buy a ticket.

I believe personal development books are just like cookbooks. If you buy a good cookbook and read the whole thing, but don't try any of the recipes, you'll never know how the recipes taste. That would seem a bit weird, right? **Funny enough, many people read books on personal finance, investing, entrepreneurship, nutrition, exercise, communication, or travel without ever trying the "recipes" or lessons the books teach.** This happens for a few reasons, which we will explore in Chapter 4, but for now, realize that you should be reading these books with the intention of implementing information from them.

Although you can make a list a mile long of problems you face while reading, all these problems stem from three major issues:

1. You're choosing the wrong books.
2. Your reading strategies are poor.
3. Your implementation strategies are poor.

If you're struggling with any (or all) of these issues, you're not alone. I've been there, and so has every reader at some point in their reading journey. No one teaches us the right way to read and implement. This book will solve those problems for you.

People often ask me, "What books do you recommend?"

At first glance, there doesn't seem to be anything wrong with this question. I am someone who has read hundreds of books and works full time in the book industry, which means that I am probably the right person to ask for a recommendation. Here's the problem: if I were to blindly suggest a book and that person were to read it, they would be reading with *my* intention *for* them instead of *their own* intention.

Instead, it surprises people when I respond with something like, "Tell me what you're looking to learn," or "Share some of your greatest challenges with me." Once we go back and forth a few times and I feel like I understand what problems someone is facing or what goals they're working on, only then can I provide a book recommendation that matches that person's individual needs.

Now, when they read the book, they are reading with *their own* power of intention.

Choosing What to Read

When I am deciding on my next book, I start by doing a personal inventory, which helps me decide what I want to read and why. Here are some example questions to ask yourself when you carry out your own inventory:

- Have I faced any major challenges recently that could have been avoided by adopting a new skill set? If so, what are the best books on that subject?

- How am I progressing on my 3-month, 6-month, and 12-month goals? Are there books that might help me achieve them faster or more efficiently?

- Will I be attending any events where the speaker or host has written any books? Do those speakers or hosts have favorite books I have not read yet?

- Are there any past or present world-changers I wish I knew more about? Have they written books or had books written about them?

- Popular books are popular for a reason. Are there any well-known books related to my personal or professional interests I have not read yet?

- Have I recently checked in with my friends, family, or mentors to see what they are reading? Do they have a good understanding of what I need to read?

- What areas of my health, wealth, or happiness need more attention?

- What books have already had a big impact on my life? Could I use a refresher? What books are similar? What books do those authors recommend?

Sometimes, people on the internet accuse me of taking the fun out of reading. As I mentioned above, I am not against reading for entertainment. When you're reading for fun, simply state that intention and write it on the inside cover to avoid any confusion.

Do I ever read just for fun? Of course, I do! Usually in the form of fiction. Although fiction is a smaller percentage of what I choose to read right now, I still find a lot of value in it. Most of the time, my intention for reading fiction is "a serving of entertainment with a side of creativity." I love the way that my brain becomes open to new ideas while reading books across random fiction genres. Plus, my vocabulary usually expands too. **Fiction is one of the only places where the impossible becomes possible with the stroke of a pen. I love that.**

Reading books also improves your attention span. In a world of instant gratification and information overload, it's nice to practice monotasking (focusing on one thing at a time). Even if you read a book for fun, you're still developing a skill that can be applied to other areas of your life.

Do I ever stop reading halfway through a book? When I first started my reading journey, I forced myself to finish every single book I started. Looking back, I don't think anyone instructed me to do this. I just felt great having read every single word on every single page. **Nowadays, I know life is too short to read books that are not going to serve their intended purpose.** Life is also too short to read bad books. For example, if I start a book to help me deal with a specific business problem and the book turns out to be on a different subject or the author doesn't seem credible, I allow myself to move on.

How much of the book do I need to read before I decide to stop? During a podcast discussion between two of my favorite authors, Tim Ferriss and Ryan Holiday, they discussed a framework you can apply in this situation called the Rule of 100. Simply start at 100 and subtract your age. The result is the number of pages you must read before you can put the book down and move on. For me, as I am writing this chapter, I am 29 years old. I know that I must read at least 71 pages of each book I pick up. The older I get, the wiser I get. The older I get, the less I must read before making that decision. As another general rule of thumb, the longer a book has been relevant, the better. Timeless wisdom is, as they say, timeless.

Do I ever read multiple books at the same time? Absolutely. I often pause one book for a few days or a few weeks, read a bit of another, and then come back to the first book. I started this habit early on and have continued it ever since. We will talk more about how to effectively read a book and take notes in Chapter 5, but for now, know that if you're organized and your intentions are clear, this is totally fine. Something interesting and unexpected happens when you read in this way that I call Book Sex.

Let's say you're reading two unrelated books. The first is a biography of one of your favorite entrepreneurs and you're reading it because you want a better understanding of how to delegate tasks to your employees. The second is on the science of intermittent fasting, and you're reading it because your mentor mentioned that fasting has really boosted her energy recently. Since both books are fresh in your mind, you start merging the two ideas together...aka Book Sex.

The result? You come up with an original and fun idea. I call these new ideas Book Babies. Instead of delegating tasks in real time, you decide to restrict your delegation to specific times during the week. This way, you can group activities together and limit the number of times you disrupt your employees' workdays. Does intermittent delegation work? I don't know. But you never would have thought of it unless you were reading both books at the same time and were open to merging their teachings together. If you're taking great notes, you can also do this intentionally by taking notes from different books and journaling about how they might work together. Try it out sometime!

Do you have to read every book you buy? No, you don't. Although I recommend buying books with intention just like I recommend reading books with intention, I recognize that life changes fast and so do your immediate needs. If you're really focused on physical fitness and buy a handful of books on the subject, you might end up finding what you need after reading only one or two. Then suddenly, another immediate need pops up and you shift your focus to addressing that. I love unread books. They represent problems you've solved or intentions you once had that have changed. You can donate them, resell them, gift them to friends, or hold on to them in case you find yourself needing them again.

Condensing Decades Into Days

Humans are funny. We think all our problems are unique to us, but the truth is that millions of people have likely faced the same problems we are currently facing. The amazing thing is that when we stop complaining about a problem and start searching for a solution, we'll find that many solutions exist. We can then go buy a book, read about those solutions, and apply them.

Sometimes, I come across people who say they'd rather figure things out themselves than rely on external help. I have never understood this. **Why experience all the pain that comes from failure when you can jump the line and learn from the mistakes of others? Not only is it faster, but it can be done from the comfort of your own home. It is both painless and efficient.** Don't be afraid to ask for help, especially from books. They can't judge you and if you order online, no one will see you searching for them in a bookstore.

Here is an example of how reading about other people's problems can help you solve your own. When I started BookThinkers, it felt like I was putting out fires every single day. Everything was a problem, because everything was new to me, and that was stressful. I started wondering, do all entrepreneurs face similar problems? I picked up books on or by some well-known entrepreneurs, people like Steve Jobs, Richard Branson, Elon Musk, and Jeff Bezos.

Once I started reading, I realized that in their earliest days, these icons of innovation faced many of the same problems I was facing. As mentioned in Chapter 1, these books condensed decades of lessons into mere days of reading. I could step back and analyze the problems I was facing from their perspectives and apply some of the solutions they had found to my own business. It was like having my own personal round table of business consultants, except of course, none of them were physically with me. We will talk more about consciously building your round table of experts in Chapter 5.

I started to wonder, where else in my life could I form a round table of experts? Could the world's best personal finance and investing gurus give me guidance on wealth? Could the world's top nutrition and fitness coaches give me guidance on health? Could the world's spiritual leaders give me guidance on inner peace and happiness? You bet they could...and they did. Hundreds of them. Could I consume billions of dollars of lessons by purchasing a $20 book? For sure.

This all sounds great, but you must be careful which books you choose to read—not all personal development books are created equally.

4. Combatting the Downsides of Self-Help

When I first started reading personal development books, I encountered a lot of skepticism from friends and family. Things like:

- "There is never any real science in those books, only pseudoscience."
- "That whole industry is a scam; you can't solve problems with books."
- "Those authors are nothing but snake-oil salespeople preying on the ignorant."

I would tell myself things like, "They're only projecting their insecurities onto me because they're scared to do any real work themselves." I do have empathy for people who cast a negative shadow on all personal development because fixed mindsets like theirs are often indicative of underlying insecurities and regrets.

Even today, after all my proven success and genuine happiness, I still hear things like, "You're just speaking into an echo chamber of other personal development people." It is unfortunate that some people feel threatened when you work on improving yourself, as if somehow, it is an attack on them.

In some instances though, my friends and family made a very good point regarding a small number of books and authors that can take you down the wrong path. When someone first starts their journey into the world of personal development, they should exercise caution. I think the 'trust but verify' approach is great advice. Most of the time, authors have spent years developing their craft, and their books' only mission is to positively impact people. In this chapter, I am going to address a few things that you should look out for when choosing which books to read so that you don't end up feeling like your time has been wasted.

Momentum Is Always Moving

Over the last five years or so, I built one of the world's largest personal development book communities, numbering over 150,000 people. During that time, I interacted with thousands of individuals as they started their reading journey. Most who joined my community fell into two buckets: a Good Mo or a Bad Mo. (Mo stands for Momentum)

Good Mo

Good Mo people start reading because they find themselves experiencing some success in life and they want to double down on that feeling. Momentum seems to be working for them and they want to make sure it stays that way. Maybe they've just gotten into a new relationship, just landed a new job, or they finally feel like they are the successful friend in their group. This person tends to feel confident, secure, and fulfilled, maybe for the first time.

When Good Mo is guiding you, personal development and self-help books are going to reinforce the positive feelings of confidence, security, and fulfillment you already have. As an example, if you've just had some success in the stock market and you decide to read a book on investing, you'll probably implement what you're learning and have even more success. This type of new reader usually has self-acceptance, will leverage what they're learning, and will align themselves with the author. If you find yourself in this bucket, great. Keep moving forward!

Bad Mo

Bad Mo people start reading because they find themselves struggling and are looking to get back on their feet. Momentum seems to be working against them and no matter what they do, they can't escape the negative spiral. Maybe their relationship has broken up, they've just lost a job, or resent how successful their friends are becoming. This person tends to feel inferior, insecure, and unfulfilled.

Unfortunately, when Bad Mo is guiding you, personal development and self-help books might reinforce those feelings of inferiority, insecurity, and lack of fulfillment. If someone is struggling financially and lacks a basic understanding of how money works, reading an advanced investing book about some guy who made millions of dollars overnight could make them feel terrible. This type of new reader usually lacks self-acceptance and will compare themselves to—as opposed to align themselves with—the author.

If you're someone who fits into the Bad Mo bucket, please build up your foundation first so that you don't double down on the negatives and end up reinforcing inadequacies. In every area of personal development and self-help, there are 'entry-level' books. Start there. Don't try to go from 0 to 100 overnight by reading complex books. Work incrementally and you'll be far more likely to enjoy the books you're reading, which will help you to reverse your negative momentum.

Reading non-fiction and personal development books is a very humbling experience. Each time you dive into a new subject, you'll discover that the world is even bigger and more complex than you thought before. Embrace this feeling and remind yourself that you're filling in those gaps and becoming a well-rounded person.

Once you feel your momentum is in a good place to align with the authors you're reading and absorb the material, be on the lookout for the rest of these roadblocks.

Progress vs. Procrastination

Readers often confuse progress with procrastination.

Here is a classic example from the world of dating. Let's say you lack the confidence to ask another person on a date. Instead of improving your confidence, the root cause of your issue, you end up reading four or five books on pickup lines and dating. While you're reading, you feel like you're making progress because you can sit back and visualize yourself confidently asking someone out. But the next time you're at the bar, you still fail to approach anyone. Failure to address the real problem leads you to read more books and before you know it, reading them feels better than actually asking anyone out. The result? You're stuck indoors every weekend reading books on dating instead of dealing with your confidence issue and going out and getting a date.

Sometimes, self-help material becomes a form of avoidance.

This happens in many ways:

- Reading about nutrition instead of eating better food.

- Reading about fitness instead of working out.
- Reading about writing instead of writing your book.
- Reading about sales instead of cold calling.
- Reading about travel instead of booking tickets.
- Reading about mindfulness instead of meditating.
- Reading about habits instead of changing your own.
- Reading about entrepreneurship instead of starting a business.
- Reading about the stock market instead of investing.

Remember, our goal as Rising Readers is to read as a form of education and behavior change, not just entertainment. This becomes tricky with some books because they are designed to create a feeling of accomplishment without encouraging real progress.

Really? Would authors intentionally do that? Well...think about it. If I can write a book that makes you feel superhuman and spend money on my course, you'll tell all your friends about it, they'll also buy my book and sign up to my course, and I'll be rich. This is a fine line for a lot of authors. You want to make the reader feel great because it improves word of mouth and how they feel about themselves, but you don't want to make them feel so good that they forget about doing the work. **If reading a book feels better than making real progress, procrastination wins.**

How can you defeat this downside of self-help? By reading with intention. We will talk about the proper ways to implement what you're reading later, but for now, remember that Rising Readers know exactly what they're reading and why they're reading it. Rising Readers know that sometimes reading becomes a form of procrastination and inhibits real progress. By being aware of that, and constantly reminding yourself of the hidden trap here, you'll avoid getting caught.

Self-Help not Shelf-Help

Some books have become so popular that people use them exclusively as status symbols or virtual meeting backgrounds. It sounds kind of funny, but I only became aware of this when people on calls started asking me, "Hey, cool background. Did you really read all these books?"

At first, noticing the books they had in their background, I thought it was a joke. "Of course! What about you?" I would respond, only to hear something back like, "Well, a few of them, but they look great, right? Doesn't this book make me look like a boss?"

Really? You have an infinite amount of wisdom and potential behind you, but you're only leveraging them as background decor? You're killing me!

When I was younger, school didn't give out participation trophies—they only handed out trophies to teams that won tournaments or kids who displayed outstanding individual effort. I used to proudly display my sports trophies in my room, and they were a reminder that hard work pays off. They encouraged me to work even harder next time.

I like to think of my books like those original sports trophies. They are Play Bigger Triggers for me. They remind me of the hard work I have put in to improve every area of my life and they motivate me to work even harder the next time I open a book. Please remember that these books are meant to be used to their fullest potential. If you're going to display books in your office, make it a rule to only display those you've read or intend on reading soon.

Personal development should be sexy, a status symbol, and represent progress. **In the same way that taking a photo standing next to someone else's Lamborghini won't make you rich, simply buying these books to display them won't solve your problems.** If your books are only there for display purposes, they become *shelf*-help instead of self-help, making your shelves look cool instead of improving your life.

Unrealistic Expectations

If you were deciding between two books, one titled *How to Make $10,000 in 30 Days*, and the other *How to Make $1,000,000 in 30 Days*, which would you choose? At first glance the latter might seem more appealing, but how realistic is the author's promise? Are they setting you up for success or are they making unrealistic claims?

In my opinion, there is nothing wrong with authors making money by selling their books, if they do it in the right way. What does "the right way" mean? To me, it means setting proper expectations and always having the reader's best interest in mind.

Just as the line between progress and procrastination can sometimes get blurry, the same thing happens with the expectations an author is setting with their book, their book title/subtitle, or the marketing of their book. There are countless books published in the US every year, which creates an incredible amount of competition for virtually every subject you could possibly write about. This pressure forces authors to one up each other and when that happens often enough, you start getting books about making a million dollars in a month.

How can you defeat this downside of self-help? Research! In a world of instant gratification, it can be challenging to pause and research a book before you purchase it, but it will do you a lot of good in the long run.

When I am researching an author for the first time, I start by checking websites like Amazon and reading through customer reviews that tell me more about the book and the author. Try to ignore the one- or two-star reviews, as those are usually written with a lot of negative emotion. Also, try to ignore the 5-star reviews because they don't typically provide much constructive criticism. **I read the three- or four-star reviews, because they contain constructive criticism and are usually written with logic instead of emotion.** Outside of web-based research, I also like asking my reading friends about different books or authors they've read. If I know someone has similar tastes and interests to mine, chances are pretty good that their feedback will go a long way in my decision-making.

There are all sorts of books out there. Books that both sell what you want and give you what you need are my preferred choice. They leverage flashy titles but deliver solid information. This leads me into my next point...

The Rule of 25%

When I started my personal development journey, I found I was reading a lot of information that made me differentiate myself from some of the people I was spending time with. Since I knew I was going to grow at the average pace of the five people I spent the most time with, I began to distance myself from those I didn't see as motivated or entrepreneurial and gravitated more toward the ones who were. We will discuss the benefits of this thinking a bit later in the book.

However, you need to be cautious of how this selective approach can be harmful too. **Not every person in your life is there to serve as motivation.** I'm not encouraging you to spend time with negative people, but to be aware that sometimes, people are just there to be friends, family, or colleagues.

Once I created the Rule of 25%, I was able to manage this distinction much more effectively. The rule states that as a Rising Reader, you should divide your time evenly between mentors, peers, mentees, and yourself.

25% Mentors: These people have had success doing exactly what you want to do in life and are willing to guide you in the right direction on your own journey. If they have helped other people achieve what you're looking to achieve, that is a great sign too. These mentors will often come in the form of authors and online courses but can also be family members, teachers, or professors.

25% Peers: Your peers are the motivated people at your side, fighting the same fight that you are and reaching for the same sorts of goals. When someone asks you, "Who are the five people you spend the most time with?" these are the people who should come to mind. Grow with them. Rise with them. We will discuss accountability and how to find these types of people in more detail later in this book.

25% Mentees: These are the people to whom you can teach what you're learning. **It is important to constantly refresh the fundamentals and teach others what you're learning since it will strengthen your own retention and understanding of the material.** There is also a reciprocal relationship between giving and receiving. The more you give (teach), the more you'll receive (learn). If you're worried you don't have enough credibility to teach others, remember you only have to be one or two steps ahead of a mentee to provide value.

25% Yourself: Spending time alone with your thoughts and feelings can be extremely transformative. It may sound a little strange, but some of my favorite memories are of times I've spent by myself, reflecting on enjoyable experiences from my past, focusing on the present, or visualizing the future. Don't underestimate how much you can learn from yourself.

The lesson? Instead of shrugging off those around you who are not motivated in the same way you are, simply change your relationship with them. Become a resource *for* them and lift them up with you on your way to becoming healthier, wealthier, and happier.

Being of value to others is one of the most important parts of being a Rising Reader. You're not just reading these books to improve your life. You're also reading them to improve the lives of those around you.

Backed by Science

The term "science" is thrown around a lot. I have heard people say that certain areas of personal development and self-help are backed by science, whereas others are not. While I tend to rely on data when making decisions, it is not always so black and white.

Is an author who references academic research studies more reliable than an author who only references their personal experiences? Sometimes, but not always. Not everything can be easily quantified. As infinitely complex human beings, we are each unique, and "science," therefore, is always changing.

It seems like half of the nutrition books out there tells you eating red meat is bad for you while the other half tells you to chow down on that steak and enjoy it. Both halves are referring to dozens of peer-reviewed academic articles coming out of the best institutions on the planet. How can this be? How can both sides be so full of proof that their recommendation is superior?

Unfortunately, that is how the world works. Scientific proof, for many areas of personal development and self-help, is situational and biased. Authors can "lie with statistics" so that their preexisting biases are proven and so their agendas can be furthered.

How can you defeat this downside of self-help? Look for data first, on both sides of the spectrum, and read the arguments for each. Without fully understanding both sides, it is hard to make an educated decision. Reading both the 'science-backed' and 'personal experience-backed' arguments is going to help as well. It's likely that each will be aware of the opposing thoughts and give you their reasoning as to why they disagree. Then, it's up to you to decide.

Of course, there are events happening in the world every single day that cannot be explained by modern science. I am not suggesting you rely on things that cannot be explained, but neither should you discredit something just because others criticize it. Sometimes, the books that created the most positive behavior change in my life were fictional stories and not backed by "science" at all.

I love personal development and self-help books. That doesn't mean I love every single book or author, but I do believe most of them have good intentions. Trust, but verify.

5. How to Read Effectively and Take Notes

How are golf and bodybuilding related to reading? I am glad you asked!

Reading and implementing personal development books is just like any skill; the more you practice, the better you'll get.

As someone who has never golfed before, I would be foolish to play with my friends who have been golfing for years and expect to beat them. It would be equally foolish to walk into a gym, hit the dumbbells and expect to have arms like Arnold Schwarzenegger after a few workouts.

Why then, would someone pick up their first couple of personal development books and expect to read fast, take great notes, and implement those notes perfectly? In this chapter, we are going to explore some of the ways I like to read and take notes so that you can practice them and get more out of the books you read.

Retaining More

Grandmaster of Memory Kevin Horsley is a world record holder of the Matrix Memorization of the first 10,000 digits of Pi, a record known as "The Everest of Memory Tests." Imagine that for a moment…memorizing 10,000 randomly sequenced digits. Before reading Kevin's bestselling book, *Unlimited Memory*, I could hardly remember my own phone number!

During a 2013 TED Talk[7], Kevin stood on stage and asked the audience who among them had read the best-selling book, *The 7 Habits of Highly Effective People*. As you can imagine, especially with an audience of learners, most people in the room raised their hands. What happened next was surprising. Kevin then asked the audience, "What are the seven habits?" and the room chuckled…presumably because no one could recall them.

Then, as if he knew this would happen, he asked the audience, **"What's the use of reading or learning anything if you can't recall what you know?** Because no matter how much you discover or experience today, its value vanishes if you forget it all tomorrow. You can only live information if you can remember it and the quality of your thinking is determined by the fact that you have remembered."

As you can imagine, the audience was silent, and so was I. I first watched a video of his speech a few years after I began my reading journey, and I was already starting to forget most of what I was reading. Why was this? At first, I wondered if our brains could only hold a certain amount of information, but it turns out that you could read for hundreds of years straight, and your brain would still have storage space left.[8] The problem, then, comes not from the amount of information you take in, but from inefficiently storing the information that you're learning.

Kevin and I became friends and started meeting weekly for virtual mentoring. One of the first things he taught me was that **repetition will**

lead to retention. It is not enough to read a book one time and expect to recall everything you've learned at the drop of a hat. You need to review that information as often as you can to truly have instant recall.

There is another benefit to constantly reviewing what you've learned, which the author and international chess master Joshua Waitzkin calls "form to leave form" or "numbers to leave numbers" in his book *The Art of Learning*. The goal of this learning strategy is to study something so deeply that your subconscious mind can act on your behalf, whether that means alerting you to opportunities to implement what you've learned or allowing you to automatically solve a problem.

Once you become a notetaker, you can review the information as often as you like. Having your biggest takeaways from every book that you read tucked away in your toolbelt and ready to use will help you become a true Rising Reader.

How often should you review your notes for better retention?

There is no simple answer to this question, but Kevin and I have talked a lot about a concept developed by German psychologist Hermann Ebbinghaus called The Forgetting Curve.[9] As you can see in the example graph below, the more often you review something, the longer you'll be able to retain it. The numbers aren't meant to be perfect, but the graph clearly shows the importance of repetition.

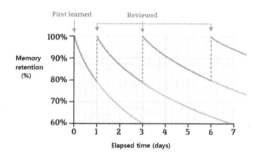

Kevin recommends reviewing information daily for a while, before moving to weekly and then monthly review sessions. Once you've studied the information so intensely that it becomes part of you, you can move on.

Taking Notes

Taking notes might be the single most important part of the reading process. Why? Because without taking notes and organizing your biggest takeaways from every book you read, you will miss opportunities to implement what you've learned. Without implementing what you've learned, reading is just a form of entertainment, not education.

My note-taking process has changed over the years, but I always find myself moving back to the basics. Each time I sit down to read, I make sure I have a pen and paper handy, and then I re-read the intention I wrote inside the cover. Instead of taking notes while I'm reading, I typically circle page numbers and bracket off the points I want to remember so that I don't lose my reading momentum. You want to avoid pivoting back and forth between two different behaviors.

Reading and taking notes are two different behaviors. Don't multitask.

Once I am done reading, I go back and write all my biggest takeaways from that reading session in a physical paper notebook. I also record the page number next to the takeaway for easy lookup later. Reviewing the information in this way enhances my understanding of the material. Remember, repetition will lead to retention.

From time to time, when something in a book strikes me as potentially life changing, I am known to tear that page out and carry it around with me. This way I can review the information dozens of times throughout the day, while increasing my retention and understanding

of the material. Whenever I post about my page-tearing on social media, the "book purists" tend to go up in arms, claiming that I am destroying the integrity of the book and disrespecting the author. I disagree, but if you're looking for alternatives, you can always snap a photo of the page, make a copy, or rewrite the information on a note card. If you want to rip *this* page out as practice, I won't stop you. Also, in my defense, ripping pages out is faster. I always put the pages back after I am done reviewing them!

Although these books can serve as Play Bigger Triggers (using the trophy metaphor from the last chapter), they are not meant to be kept in pristine condition on your shelves. **I like my books to look like they've been through war, filled with notes, highlighter, torn pages, and coffee stains.** These books are tools in your toolbelt, not pieces of art that must be protected by a six-foot barrier and velvet rope. I hope that by the time you're finished with *this* book, it fits the description above. I am the type of author who would take that as a compliment.

Once I finish a book, I will record my top five to 10 takeaways into an online notebook. My favorite online notebook is Evernote, which I've used for a long time—I really like its search and tagging functionalities. I have lost physical notebooks before, so having the information backed up online is important to me. When I rewrite my notes and store them online, I group them into categories like Action Items, Quotes, General Notes, More Research Required, Further Reading, or Miscellaneous. By leveraging Evernote, you can also add tags to your notes so that if you want to search your system for all takeaways related to "money," you can quickly work your way through the notes you've taken across many different books.

The reason I limit the number of takeaways I add to my online notebook is to remain intentional about what I'm going to implement. Sometimes this means choosing the 20% of my notes that have 80% of the potential impact for me. We will dive deeper into the 80/20 Rule in Chapter 10. I remember reading *Think and Grow Rich* by Napoleon Hill for the first time and coming away with over 100 notes. That was overwhelming because I knew there was no way I could review and implement them all every day without losing interest.

For me, audiobooks follow a similar process, except that I take notes in my phone's notes section since I don't usually have a notebook handy. If I am driving, I pull over and jot my notes or voice-to-text a summary of what I just heard so that I can go back and look up the actual text later. After that, I follow the same process of recording my top takeaways into Evernote.

E-books have been growing on me recently. With most e-books, you can highlight sections of the book, add your own notes, and export everything to your email. However, I still enjoy writing my biggest takeaways with pen and paper so that I can have that intimate, repetitive experience of consolidating what I've read. If you're new to reading, that might sound quirky, but over time, you'll know exactly what I mean.

Schedule Reading Time

I have had many people tell me, "Hey Nick, reading sounds great, but I can never find the time to sit down and focus on a book." I usually reply with something like, "That's unfortunate. Question for you. If I were to give you $10,000 to read a book by next week, do you think you could find a way to make it happen?" Quickly, they respond with a "Yes!" not realizing they've proven the following point:

If your reason to read (your intention) is big enough, you will find the time to read.

You've already learned that Rising Readers read with intention, but they also proactively schedule reading time into their calendars. This is important because reading is rarely life or death and will usually fall down the priority list as each day pulls you into its whirlwind of chaos.

Nowadays, I sit down at the beginning of each week and try to plan at least 10 hours of reading time into my calendar. Sometimes, that means one hour of reading each weekday and another five hours spread over the weekend, and other times it means an entire day of reading on the weekend. My favorite place to read is on airplanes. Airplanes naturally minimize environmental distractions and don't provide many brain-boosting alternatives to reading. Boston to Los Angeles? No problem. That's four solid hours of reading time with a two-hour nap or movie in between. Yes, I still enjoy movies!

Bookend Your Days

By controlling my morning routine and my evening routine, aka 'bookending' my days, I have a much better chance at controlling the middle of my day. Yes, I am one of those people with a long morning routine full of meditations, affirmations, and the occasional ice bath or sauna. As you might have guessed, I also schedule in some reading time—usually around 15 minutes—every morning and evening to ensure I keep up the momentum.

You may find yourself scratching your head, asking yourself, "How in the world am I going to fit 15 minutes of reading into my schedule every morning and every evening?"

Most people can resonate with the following outline of an average day:

- 8 hours of sleep
- 8 hours of work
- 2 hours of meals
- 2 hours of family time

How many hours is that? Twenty. Where in the world do those other four hours go on weekdays?

Studies show that the average American watches three hours of television per day and spends over two hours on social media. Hmmm... I wonder if those people are even working eight hours?

15 Minutes Will Change Your Life

Remember...

- 15 minutes of reading = roughly 10 pages for beginners
- 10 pages in the morning + 10 pages in the evening = 20 pages/day
- 20 pages/day * 5 weekdays = 100 pages/week
- 100 pages/week * 52 weeks = 5,200 pages/year
- 5,200 pages/year ÷ 250 pages/book = **OVER 20 BOOKS**

By replacing 15 minutes of your morning Instagram scrolling and the first 15 minutes of your evening Netflix session with reading, you can improve 20 different areas of your life in the next year.

Entertainment-to-Education Ratio

This ratio is a simple way to compare the amount of time you spend on entertainment with the amount of time you spend on education on a weekly basis. What is the purpose of tracking this? If you aren't continually measuring something, it is hard to improve it. Once you know your ratio, you can start making progress against it.

Let's say I calculate this ratio for a friend. I would start by asking what kinds of entertainment they consume on a regular basis. Netflix? Social media? Okay great. I would encourage you to follow along and write your own numbers down. Be realistic when estimating these:

- 3 hours of television entertainment/day = 21 hours/week
- 2 hours of social media entertainment/day = 14 hours/week
- Total entertainment = 35 hours/week

Next, I'd ask about what kinds of self-education they engage with on a regular basis. It might look something like this:

- 0.5 hours of reading education/day = 3.5 hours/week
- 0.5 hours of audio education/day = 3.5 hours/week
- Total education = 7 hours/week

The result? A 5:1 entertainment-to-education ratio. My friend is spending five hours on entertainment for every hour that they are spending on self-education. That doesn't mean anything objectively, other than they are living under their potential, but now you can clearly see where this person's priorities are. I recommend they start tracking these numbers on a weekly basis and start working toward a 1:1 ratio. I advise you to do the same. If you've been following along and your ratio is education-heavy, you can pat yourself on the back because that is very rare these days.

While writing this, I feel a strange need to remind you that I am not a robot and I still enjoy watching Netflix, vacationing, and exploring the world. It seems kind of backward to me, but our society has found a way to cast a negative light on people who delay gratification and spend time working on themselves. Part of the Rising Reader mentality is to reverse this narrative and make reading sexy again. Personal development should never be demonized.

As Jocko Willink reminds us in his book, *Extreme Ownership*, "Discipline equals freedom."[10] It is counterintuitive, but true. The more discipline you exercise in life, the more freedom you'll have. For example, when you practice discipline throughout the workday and minimize distractions, you complete your work faster and create more free time.

Here is my version of that quote: **The more you focus on "boring" educational stuff, the more "entertaining" your life becomes. The opposite is unfortunately true as well. The more you focus on "entertaining" stuff, the more "boring" your life becomes.**

Funny how that works…

Who Will Sell More?

Let's say you and your neighbor are both sales professionals, working for the same company. In the past 12 months, you've sold the same amount of new business.

Your neighbor is hungry to sell more, so he decides to implement the reading schedule above and read the 20 best sales books of all time over the next 12 months. These books teach your neighbor advanced prospecting, persuasive communication, and closing and negotiation skills, all of which are important in your shared role. You, on the other hand, are complacent and decide to watch Netflix instead.

Who sells more throughout the next year? You or your neighbor?

Winner winner chicken dinner. Loser loser Netflix chooser!

If 15 minutes, two times per day, is not enough to satisfy your hunger for self-education, I would recommend scheduling larger amounts of time into your calendar.

My Thursday Night Rum & Coke Reading Strategy

During my senior year of college, my friends would ask me to go out and drink $1 rum & Cokes until the sun came up, and for a while, I did—until I found out that drinking kills your brain cells.

Does alcohol destroy brain cells? No, not technically. But I can tell you that thinking it did removed any FOMO (fear of missing out) that may have tried entering my brain.

You know how some people are fueled by waking up early and accomplishing great things before their competition is up? Well, I was fueled by creating new neural pathways instead of destroying brain cells. From that point on, I dedicated all my Thursday evenings to reading instead of partying.

I am SO happy that I made that sacrifice years ago and chose to read.

As a rule of thumb, when you're facing a tough decision like going out to drink or staying in to read, ask yourself, **"When I look back on this decision tomorrow, which option will leave me feeling more fulfilled?"** This one simple question helps me to minimize short-term destructive behavior and maximize long-term helpful behavior. More on that in Chapter 10: Delayed Gratification.

Reading Hygiene

First and foremost, make sure you brush your book covers and floss your bookshelves!

I am kidding...unless you're into that. Reading hygiene means making sure you're setting yourself up for a healthy reading session. Some of these items might seem trivial, but I promise that each one of them makes a positive difference.

Environment. In what kind of environment are you most effective? My ideal reading environment has a few characteristics. First, I love reading in peace and quiet. If I can't have that, I need the ability to play quiet instrumental music. I am not someone who prides himself on being able to multitask or work in a chaotic, noisy environment, so I always try to find reading environments that offer minimal distractions. Nothing stops your flow like a kid running into the room or a waiter talking your ear off. Decent lighting and a relaxed seating arrangement are nice too. You don't want to sacrifice your eyesight by reading in a dimly lit room or strain your neck by reading in an uncomfortable chair.

Posture. In *Cues* by Vanessa Van Edwards, I learned that your body position impacts your mood and energy more than you'd think. For instance, if you lean forward, your mind becomes more engaged in the material you're reading, whereas if you slouch backward, you can become tired very quickly. Another example is that a closed body signals a closed mind. If you slump your shoulders and become closed off to the book, your mind will become closed off too. You want to read in an open position, with your shoulders back and your head up, so that you can have an open mind.

Mood. Even the best cup of coffee in the world will taste bitter if you're in a bitter mood. Before I even pick up a book, I make sure that I feel balanced, eager to learn, and optimistic. If you're feeling negative or uninspired, you might be better off dealing with that first. There is an opportunity cost to reading in a bad mood because you might shrug off something that could change your life.

Energy. My favorite time of day to read is mid-morning, right after a great workout, which is when I have the most energy. When I compound my high energy levels with some cognitive enhancers like a cup of coffee, I am ready to devour a book. If instead, I tried to read for an extended period at the end of a demanding day, I would be a mess. If reading means a lot to you, prioritize it so that it matches your highest energy levels.

Intention. Whenever I sit down to read, I love to review my intention written inside the front cover. What is your intention for reading *this* book? Reviewing that intention will help you filter what you're learning so that you can look for the biggest opportunities to implement what you really need.

Notes. One of my issues with audiobooks is that I typically listen to them in the car and that means that I can't take world-class notes. We touched on this earlier in the chapter, but for now, remember that having a pen and paper handy will do wonders for you. Always have a fresh notebook within arm's reach so that you can transcribe your biggest takeaways after each reading session.

Success. What does a successful reading session look like? By defining this up front, you have a goal to shoot for. This way, you don't read aimlessly, and you can feel good about what you read instead of wondering if it was enough. The three most common goal formats for reading are:

- I want to read at least X pages.
- I want to read for at least X minutes.
- I want to read until I learn at least X new things.

Imagine trying to read after a long, stressful day where your boss dampened your mood, and now the TV is distracting you. Even worse, you misplaced your notebook and you forgot to refocus by reviewing your intention. That might sound extreme, but I am sure many readers can relate. Rising Readers pay attention to these factors because there is a very clear opportunity cost to avoiding them...bad hygiene.

Slow and Steady Does NOT Win the Race (while reading)

Have you ever found yourself a few pages into a book and you suddenly realize you're daydreaming about something totally unrelated? Of course, you have! It happens to all of us.

In his book *Limitless*, Jim Kwik teaches us that by increasing reading speed, we can minimize distractions and improve comprehension. Jim says that reading is just like driving a car. The faster you drive, the more focus you need and the less daydreaming you can do.

When you're reading slowly, you're not taking advantage of your brain's full capabilities. Our brains are literally supercomputers and can handle much more than we typically give them credit for. The faster you read, the less distracted you'll be, and the more books you'll read in less time.

If you want to take this a step further, Jim recommends reducing the amount of subvocalization that you do. Subvocalization, or silent speech, is the act of inaudibly articulating the words to yourself as you read. As Jim explains, we can only subvocalize as fast as we can speak, which is much slower than we can read.

Build a Bookbelt to Fix Any Problem

You know how construction workers wear a toolbelt, ready to grab a hammer when they see a nail, or a screwdriver when they see a screw? Books do the same thing for me. There are plenty of times where I learn something in a book that is not immediately or directly applicable to my life, so I tuck it away until I find a use for it. My metaphorical toolbelt has come in handy more times than I can count. In the spirit of being a Rising Reader, I decided to refer to my toolbelt as a Bookbelt instead.

Here is a real-life example of how you can leverage this Bookbelt metaphor. Let's say you just bought a new car and, in the process, found out that you're a terrible negotiator. Fueled by your experience, you decide to read an excellent book on negotiation. After finishing the book and taking amazing notes, you realize you're not often in situations where you can leverage your new skills. That's okay. Tuck these skills into your Bookbelt so that you know exactly where to find them when you need them.

Over time, regularly review the tool (your notes) and make sure you're ready to use it the next time you need it, which you will, eventually. New house? New job? You can just reach for your negotiation tool. Pull out your notes, review and practice the night before you need them, and you'll be prepped and ready to negotiate.

If you're feeling overwhelmed by a problem, would you rather face it alone, or with the right toolkit? I find it comforting that these books are always available to me and right by my side. Life is too complex to navigate effectively without a good Bookbelt and good counsel.

Who Sits at Your Round Table?

When I was a kid, I was fascinated by kings and knights and dragons. Naturally, I learned about the Knights of the Round Table, a noble group of men who consulted King Arthur on matters of great importance. Well, it might sound crazy, but I am always expanding my own round table. Whenever I am dealing with a big problem, I ask myself, "Who would be the best person to help me with this?" If someone comes to mind, I will review my notes from their book and then filter my thought processes through their tried-and-tested decision-making frameworks.

No, this exchange doesn't always come in the form of a picturesque daydream where I consult the world's most successful problem-solvers around an ornate table, but sometimes it does.

This metaphor pairs well with the vision I have of a Rising Reader, sword in one hand, book in the other, ready to slay dragons (problems). Plus, where else can you recruit world-class mentors and have lifelong relationships with them for $20?

Please STOP and review this book!

If you're enjoying this book and finding value in what you're learning, please leave a review on the platform where you purchased it.

There is NO better compliment to an author than a positive book review.

Positive reviews help books rank better on the platforms that sell them and give potential readers more insight on what they can expect to learn.

Plus, a review creates some good karma and who couldn't use a little of that? Thank you!

PART II:
Habits and Behavior Change

6. The Compound Effect

I have thrown a lot at you, and we are still early in the book. As we discussed in Chapter 4, this type of information can often feel daunting if you're new to the space.

Truth is, although I felt extremely optimistic about my future when I started reading personal development books, I was also overwhelmed by the size of the task. Changing your entire life is no small or easy feat. Then, to my relief, I found a simple strategy that helped calm my mind and reframe my approach to implementing everything I was learning.

It goes by many names: the compound effect, the cumulative effect, the slight edge, atomic habits, tiny habits, baby steps, the 1% principle, exponential progression, delayed gratification...etc. I choose to call it The Compound Effect because I was introduced to the concept by a book of the same name, written by Darren Hardy.

At the basis of all these terms is one simple concept: small steps in the right direction, repeated over a long period of time, will lead to huge rewards.

1% Improvements

Too often, society convinces us that massive success requires massive action, but that is not true.

Massive action is nice, but you need to build yourself up to it. Instead, let's walk through the impact of a 1% improvement. The purpose of what I am about to show you is that personal development does not have to be time consuming or intimidating.

Math was never my favorite subject, but the following equations might be the most empowering thing you'll ever read.[11] Check this out:

- Scenario 1: $1.00 \wedge 365 = 1.00$
- Scenario 2: $1.01 \wedge 365 = 37.78$
- Scenario 3: $0.99 \wedge 365 = 0.03$

In Scenario 1, you take an action (1.00) and repeat it for 365 days without any change. The result? Nothing. You stay the same. This is what it looks like when people are going through life on cruise control, hoping for change, but doing nothing to create it.

In Scenario 2, you take that same action, apply a 1% improvement to it daily (1.01), and repeat it for 365 days. The result? A 37-fold improvement! That is exponential progression at its finest! This is what it looks like when people apply a growth mindset to different areas of their life, knowing that over time, it will compound into something special.

In Scenario 3, you take that same action, but instead, decrease it by 1% daily (0.99), and repeat it for 365 days. The result? You're basically at 0 now. This is an extremely important equation because it shows us that compounding can work in both ways, either for us, or against us. This is what it looks like when someone lets their standards slip and becomes stuck in the negative momentum.

Flying Out of Control

One of my all-time favorite examples of The Compound Effect can be found in the air. Let's say you're a pilot, flying from Los Angeles to New York City. While you're taking off, the nose of the plane is pointed 1% off course, to the south. This small, almost unnoticeable adjustment will compound over and over while you're flying. The result? You'll end up over 100 miles south of New York City, somewhere in the middle of Delaware. Your passengers are not going to be happy! Check it out:

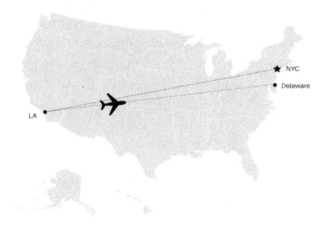

As we fly through life, if we repeat 1% improvements, we become wildly different people. When we repeat 1% decreases, we also become wildly different people. These slight adjustments during takeoff will change your life as they compound day after day, month after month, and year after year. It is time to take control of your habits.

Winning the Race

I noticed something interesting while watching the Summer Olympic Games. There are dozens of different sports played during the Olympics, but most of them are decided by a very small margin. Sprinters and swimmers win by a fraction of a second. Soccer and basketball games are usually decided by a point or two.

Are the gold medalists 10 times better than the other competitors? No, of course not. But they do get 10 times the reward. They are typically the ones who get the glory, the sponsorship deals, the book deals, the speaking gigs, etc. Do you want to know what they are? They are 1% better.

Where did that 1% come from? Well, in the thousands of hours that lead up to an event, it's the small things that make a difference. Picture a sprinter, running one extra lap on the track after everyone else's workouts are finished. Picture a swimmer spending one extra minute working on her form before getting in the pool. Picture a soccer player asking the goalkeeper to stay late, so he can work on his penalty kick. Picture a basketball player shooting one extra free throw after practice.

The lesson here?

The best in the world, in any discipline, aren't superheroes. They are committed to constant improvement, and they are willing to work 1% harder, every day.

Small Steps in Health, Wealth, and Happiness

If you're not planning on taking a pilot's exam or competing in the next Olympics, you might be wondering, "What activities can I start making 1% improvements on?"

The correct answer is, almost everything you do. Let's look at some of the basic ways you can improve just one area of your health—sleep:

- Less blue light exposure near bedtime (no scrolling!)
- Going to bed at a regular time
- Room-darkening shades and an eye mask
- Lowering your bedroom temperature
- Lowering the temperature of your mattress
- Weighted blanket and a better pillow
- Bi-neural noise machine
- Sleep supplements
- Waking up at a regular time
- Early morning sunlight exposure

These almost effortless changes in your sleep routine can offer you a lifetime of benefits.

Chances are that no one else will notice the changes you're making. Remember, oftentimes it will take years for these changes to lead to any noticeable outcomes.

Where you are today is the result of the habits you've been indulging in over the last few years. It's never too late to start changing your behavior.

The Butterfly Effect

Okay, so you're sleeping better. Now what?

The benefits of improving your sleep are seemingly endless, but my favorite is an increase in energy. Energy is one of those concepts that is difficult to measure, but you know what it feels like to wake up in the morning after a great night's sleep, full of life, and ready to conquer your day.

Let's say that, hypothetically, this improved daily energy leads to more productivity at work. Over the next couple of months, your improved productivity catches the attention of your boss, and you're given more responsibility. This additional responsibility comes with a pay raise, and a welcome boost to your income. You can use that income in a variety of ways, but since you're reading about personal finance, you choose to snowball some of your debt and get ahead of your college loans.

Since you're loving your new energy, you start to wonder if there are other ways to improve it even further. This never would have occurred to you if you hadn't decided to improve your sleep habits, since your energy wasn't something you ever gave much attention to in the first place. You start researching the connection between your diet and your energy and decide to start eating healthier and lose those 10lbs you've been complaining about for years.

Look at you now! Who would have thought that by improving your sleep, you'd end up getting a raise at work and losing some weight. This concept is often referred to as The Butterfly Effect[12] or The Ripple Effect,[13] when one action leads to a string of other actions that you didn't foresee. However, The Butterfly Effect is unpredictable, and you must be careful because, just like the momentum we learned about in Chapter 4, it works in both directions. You've probably heard stories of how it can compound against someone too.

Things are going well, but suddenly, your company goes out of business, and you lose your job. You loved that job. To distract yourself, you start watching more TV. Since companies like Netflix are literally engineered to steal your attention, you start binging shows late into the night and end up losing sleep. That lost sleep decreases your energy. Your energy slump isn't helping you find a new job, which perpetuates your feelings of inadequacy. You stop eating healthy, which you previously took pride in, simply because you don't have the desire to pay attention to it. You gain weight. This now lowers your energy even further...etc. This momentum is dangerous, and you need to pay attention when it begins to creep in.

Embracing the concept of exponential progression—The Compound Effect—and applying it to my own life took away my feelings of being overwhelmed. The strategies you read in this book can be accomplished with small modifications to your existing behavior. They're almost imperceptible.

I am sure there is something in your life, a big project, or a major bucket list item, that you've wanted to achieve for a long time. Start by determining the smallest first step imaginable and do it now. These big goals don't have to be tackled with big actions, just small steps in the right direction.

The Matthew Effect

Do you remember the golf metaphor that kicked off Chapter 5? In summary, it shows us that reading and applying information is a skill that can be improved through practice.

This is reinforced by a concept called The Matthew Effect, first coined in 1968 by sociologists Robert K. Merton and Harriet Zuckerman.[14] The biblical Gospel of Matthew, chapter 25 verse 29 reads, "For whoever has will be given more, and they will have an abundance. Whoever does not have, even what they have will be taken from them."[15] In other words: the rich get richer, and the poor get poorer.

When we take this effect and apply it to knowledge, we could say that the smarter get smarter, and the dumber get dumber. If you and Warren Buffett read the same investing magazine, who will gain more insight? Warren will. Why? Because he has a foundation of existing knowledge from reading and investing that is larger than yours and therefore can make more sense of the magazine's value.

This is important because the more you learn, the more you *can* learn.

Sometimes, I will read a book for a second or third time, years after the first reading, and find a completely new set of takeaways. This happens because my foundation of knowledge is constantly expanding, and I can interpret what I am learning through a new lens, absorbing more from the book.

Not only can you learn more, but you can learn faster. By implementing all of the strategies outlined in this book and practicing them across many books, you'll become a learning machine.

7. Understanding Habits

Where you are today is the result of the repetitive actions you've been undertaking for the past few years.

These repetitive actions, also known as habits, have created everything you know, everything you do, and everything you are today. The food you consume, the exercise (or lack thereof) you partake in, the work you focus on, the friends you connect with, and the books you read have created the person that you are in this moment. The person reading this book.

The good news is that the person you will be in a few years is being created today by those same repetitive actions. You have the power to improve those habits and create the future 'you' of your choice.

The goal of this chapter is to help you create more awareness of your habits and give you the tools you need to uninstall bad habits so that you can close the gap between where you are now and where you want to be. Let's dive in!

Activator, Action, Outcome

When I teach habit reforming to other people, I use the following elements: an activator, an action, and an outcome. Let's take a deeper look at each of these elements:

Activators generally fall into a few different categories, such as locations, people, emotional states, times of day, or other actions. These activators have been created from past experiences, are processed automatically, and lead to actions. For example, being at a movie theater (activator: location) activates the desire to eat popcorn, or a stressful memory (activator: emotional state) activates the desire to smoke a cigarette. These activators vary in power, but unless they are consciously disrupted or rerouted, they will continue leading to a preinstalled action.

Actions are the behaviors you're looking to change or reinforce, and they are triggered by an activator. Each action has a short-term outcome and a long-term outcome.

Outcomes are the reason your brain decides to remember the previous steps. The outcome provides reinforcement for the behavior, making it more likely that you will default to that behavior again in the future. These outcomes might feel like rewards in the short term, but oftentimes, they are more like handicaps in the long term, holding you back from becoming your ideal self. Popcorn feels great in the moment but leaves you bloated after you're done. Smoking cigarettes immediately feeds your craving but increases your risk of getting cancer years down the road. Do these actions align with who you're looking to become over the next five or 10 years?

I like to think of this automated loop as a biological system, designed to work in your favor. Remember, our brains are always trying to seek pleasure and avoid pain. As humans evolved and gained more day-to-day control over our external environment, these systems went from saving our lives (see a tiger, run from a tiger, stay alive) to stressing us out (see an Instagram post that makes you feel stressed, smoke a cigarette, feel relief from Instagram).

Now that you have a better understanding of the variables associated with your habits, let's talk about how you can install systems that align with your long-term goals and uninstall systems that don't.

Restate, Isolate, and Eliminate Objections

When I was first running my house painting business in college, I had a tough time selling my services. I was taught to go door-to-door and schedule a time with homeowners where I could come back, walk around their house with them, and generate an official proposal to paint what needed to be painted. I was usually efficient at setting up these free estimates, but I struggled with closing the deal and collecting signatures.

That was until my sales mentor, Kurt, taught me how to handle objections. Kurt showed me that the real sale doesn't start until someone says no, and that homeowners were usually hiding their true objections so that they didn't hurt my feelings. I learned that if I could identify their true objection, I would have a better chance at closing the deal.

The framework was called "Restate, Isolate, and Eliminate" and it worked beautifully:

- Step 1: Restate the objection(s).
- Step 2: Isolate the objection(s) with an if/then statement.
- Step 3: Eliminate the real objection(s).
- Step 4: Close the deal.

Here is an example of how it worked. When I would go for a close, I would often hear something like, "Thank you, but the price seems kind of high. I will think about it and get back to you." Recalling the framework, I would **restate** the objection out loud. "Okay, you believe that the price seems high." Next, comes the **if/then statement**. I would try to isolate the objection by asking, "If price was not a concern, then would you be willing to move ahead with the deal?"

If the homeowner said, "Yes," great! Now I just needed to prove my value and **eliminate** the price objection. Most of the time, though, it was at this point that the real objection comes out. They would say something like, "Well, now that you mention it, I am also unsure if a bunch of college students can really get the job done without fooling around." Again, I would restate the objections out loud and then try to isolate them. "Thank you for your honesty. If price was not a concern and if I was able to show you that my painters are professional and hardworking, would you then be willing to move forward with my proposal?" Once the customer agrees and you're able to eliminate the objection, you can go in and close the deal.

Do you see how this framework helped me really get to the root cause of the objections?

Without it, I was working to solve objections that were not really objections, which resulted in no business. By isolating and listing out the homeowners' real concerns, I could transition to the final stage of the framework and eliminate their real objections. There are entire books written on the different ways to handle objections and close deals, but the core of every sales philosophy is closing the gap between where your customer is and where they want to be. By showing homeowners referrals, samples of past work, our certifications, and examples of how our competitors would price the same deals, my closing ratio went way up.

Trying to change your actions and behaviors without realizing that they are caused by external triggers is just like trying to solve an objection that is not a real objection. If you don't find the weeds and pull them out by their roots, they will find a way to sneak back into your life.

Now that you understand how this framework can boost sales, let's apply it to changing our habits.

Restate, Isolate, and Eliminate Bad Habits

Have you ever found yourself halfway through a bag of Spicy Nacho Doritos a few days after you've promised yourself you're never eating them again? I have. Multiple times. It was always the strangest feeling because I knew I wanted to give them up, yet I wouldn't become aware I was eating them until I was halfway through the bag.

Was that behavior so ingrained in me that every Sunday while watching football, I would walk to the pantry, grab a bag, walk back to the couch, and start eating them on autopilot?

Yes, unfortunately, it was.

Thankfully, I have never struggled with my weight, but I still knew that those Doritos were not healthy. They tasted great and made me happy in the moment, but each snacking session left me feeling bloated and lazy for hours after the bag was empty.

So, what did I do? I applied a slightly modified version of the aforementioned sales framework to eliminate the bad habit and yank it out by the roots. It looked like this:

- Step 1: Restate the bad habit (and why it's bad) out loud to create awareness.
- Step 2: Isolate the activator with an if/then statement.
- Step 3: Eliminate the activator so that the bad habit goes away.

Here's how that process played out for me:

Step 1: Restate

During those brief moments of awareness when you realize you're participating in a bad habit, it's important to restate the behavior and its consequences out loud. **By doing this, you're consciously disrupting the behavior**. Otherwise, your sense of awareness will pass, and you'll resume the bad activity.

Picture me sitting on the couch with my hand in the bag. I suddenly become aware of what I'm doing. I stop, stand up, and take a step back to create some distance from the bag. I restate the bad habit out loud by saying something like, "I am choosing to snack on Doritos even though they make me feel bloated and lazy!" Each time I restated the bad habit out loud, I would immediately stop snacking and put the Doritos away.

Step 2: Isolate

Next, you're going to isolate the activator that's causing your bad behavior with an if/then statement. Start by listing all the potential triggers and then temporarily eliminate them one at a time to see if it solves your problem. Remember, activators usually fall into these categories: locations, people, emotional states, time of day, or other actions and they cause your bad habit to repeat itself.

For the Doritos habit, I listed these potential activators:

- My living room (location where I watched football)
- My pantry (location where I kept the Doritos)
- My family (people who I watched football with)
- My excitement while watching football (emotional state)
- My hunger for snack food (emotional state)
- Sunday afternoons (time of day)
- Watching football (action proceeding the snacking)

Once I listed the variables individually, I tried eliminating them temporarily, one at a time, to see if I still wanted to eat Doritos.

The result? I found that having them in the pantry and being hungry for snack food were the activators causing me to eat them. Temporarily removing activators is one thing, but permanently removing them is another.

Step 3: Eliminate

After stating your bad habit out loud and isolating the activators, you need to eliminate them.

My favorite strategies for doing this are Removing the Activator and/or Replacing the Automated Action.

Removing the Activator is exactly what it sounds like. Once you've isolated the activator using the techniques above, you simply remove it from your life. In the example above, the root cause was the availability of the Doritos and my feelings of early afternoon hunger.

To remove the availability of the Doritos, I simply had to stop purchasing them. Was it hard to avoid purchasing Doritos at the supermarket? Not at all. However, I sure got some funny looks when I passed the snack food aisle and started publicly harassing the Doritos bags.

Since the other activator was my early afternoon hunger, I decided to eat bigger lunches so that I didn't feel any hunger or temptation to snack during afternoon football games. This was also easy, since we usually cook in large portions at my house.

Replacing the Automated Action comes in handy if you can't remove the activator. Let's say you live with someone who loves Doritos, and they are not willing to stop buying them. Well, instead of moving out, you can start creating a new relationship between your afternoon munchies and a healthier snack food.

Eventually, you'll be automatically associating Sunday football with carrots and celery. This takes time and can be a struggle but is worth it if you cannot remove the root cause activator.

There is one final strategy that has worked for me, which is Amplifying the Negative Outcome. Bad habits have bad long-term outcomes. The short-term rewards are great, but the long-term consequences are always damaging. The goal of this strategy is to focus on the impact of the negative outcome by spending more time thinking about it. In the case of the Doritos, I grabbed a pen and paper and did the following math:

- 1,200 calories/bag[16] * 2 bags/week = 2,400 calories/week
- 2,400 calories/week * 52 weeks/year = 124,800 calories/year
- 124,800 calories/year * 5 years = 624,000 calories in 5 years
- 1 pound of body fat = about 3,500 calories
- 624,000 ÷ 3,500 = 178lbs of fat over 5 years

No. More. Doritos.

Meditate on it until the thought of Doritos makes you run in the other direction. You'd have to work out *a lot* to burn off 178lbs of fat. Visualize 178lbs of fat each time you pick up the Doritos bag and imagine your body starting to feel bloated. My guess is that you'll stop buying them immediately. I know I did. These techniques really work.

Sometimes people ask me how long it takes to uninstall a bad habit. After reviewing dozens of books and case studies on the subject, it is still hard to say definitively. Some popular studies show 21 days while others show 66 days. Long story short, it depends on variables like repetition, intensity, and time. One thing I know is that the quicker you can accurately identify a bad habit's activator and remove it, the quicker you can replace it with something that serves you better.

Now that you have a good understanding of how habits work and how to remove bad habits, let's talk about how to install good habits. Consider this: hard work beats talent when talent doesn't work hard especially if the hard worker has better habits.

Throughout the next chapter, we are going to discuss the strategies I have used to implement over 100 healthy, wealthy, and happy habits into my life.

8. Success Buddies

I picked up *The Compound Effect* by Darren Hardy for the first time in 2017. Even today, it's still in my top five most impactful books.

I had been recommending books to a close group of friends and one of them, Joseph, decided to read this one at the same time as me. As we progressed through the book, we both found the section about tracking your activity and accountability groups fascinating.

Since we had both been struggling with how to implement what we were reading, Joseph suggested we follow the book's recommendation and start our own accountability group. We followed the templates and created our very own activity trackers. As two people who were looking to drastically improve our lives, this was a no-brainer. We decided to call this group Success Buddies. The name has stuck ever since.

After meeting for a few weeks, Joseph introduced the concept to a couple of our other friends. One of them, Tony, really took to the idea and Joseph started meeting with him each week as well. As the weeks progressed, we added more functions to our activity trackers and created something a little more advanced. I started by tracking basic health and fitness goals like the number of workouts I was completing per week.

Eventually, we all merged, and formed a group of three. **Over the following year, we met every single week and each of us made massive progress in our lives.** Throughout that time, we had a handful of people join the group but eventually fizzle out. We developed high expectations for each other and if anyone repeatedly failed to meet those expectations, they were out.

I finally had a group of people who were constantly holding me to higher expectations and challenging me to become a better version of myself, week in, week out.

I needed that focus. I was reading about setting bigger goals, working smarter, and expanding my vision of what was possible. Yet I was struggling to stay motivated when I hit roadblocks set up by some of my family and friends, who would say things like, "You are already achieving so much for your age. You should enjoy your weekends instead of focusing on self-improvement." They believed that focusing on personal development type material was another form of "work" and no one likes "work," right?

I see so many people become motivated and then get shot down by the people around them and lose their momentum. Not everyone wants to see you succeed. My accountability group stopped that negative energy from influencing me.

I was reading like a madman during this period and each time I would find something that I wanted to implement into my life, I would plug it right into my activity tracker and tell my group about it.

Although we only met once a week for an hour or two, we kept up a constant group chat where we could share wins throughout the week and push group members who seemed to be slacking, since we could review everyone's trackers in real time.

The original Success Buddies crew has faded away—but two new groups have taken its place.

When people ask how I can successfully implement so much from the books I read, I tell them it all starts with my accountability groups. The ingredients are simple:

- Two to three friends who want to make progress in their lives
- A shared activity tracker that measures weekly goals
- Weekly calls to review our activity and to hold each other accountable

How to Structure Goals

I can't write a full chapter on accountability without talking about how to structure goals. The better you structure your goals, the better your accountability partner(s) can assist you.

I recommend combining the **SMART goal formula** with **Intention**. Here's what that formula means for me:

S stands for Specific. When setting your goal, avoid ambiguity. Instead of a vague goal like, "I want to travel next year," say something specific like, "I want to travel to Peru this year with my girlfriend." Be as precise as possible.

M stands for Measurable. Having measurable goals allows you to track your progress. Remember, you can't manage progress if you're not measuring progress. Ask yourself questions like, "How will I know when my goal is accomplished?" In the example above, you will know if you traveled to Peru this year or not.

A stands for Achievable. Is your goal realistic and achievable? If you're limited on time and funds, setting a goal to visit 25 countries in the next year is not achievable. The risk of setting unachievable goals is that you'll become discouraged and end up achieving less than you would have with a more reasonable goal.

R stands for wRitten. This one is a little bit of a cheat, but hey, it works. To me, wRitten means documented. Thoughts written down become real goals, otherwise, they remain just thoughts. Oftentimes people put Later in this chapter, you'll be learning how to create an activity tracker just like the one I use so that you'll always have a place to wRite your goals.

T stands for Time Frame. Without an expiration date, your goal has no urgency. Saying, "I want to travel" makes it too easy to procrastinate and consistently push your actions off until "tomorrow." By adding the element of a time frame, others can easily hold you accountable. This week, this month, and this year are all reasonable time frames. I have learned that the shorter your time frame, the more likely you are to achieve your goals. **Too many New Year's resolutions are never achieved because the time frame is too large.**

"Travel to Peru this year with my girlfriend" is Specific, Measurable, Attainable, wRitten, and bound by Time. What is it missing? Your why! Creating a goal without a strong why is like reading without intention.

Intention. To add intention, simply use the word "*because*" at the end of your SMART goal. It could look like this: "Travel to Peru this year with my girlfriend *because* Machu Picchu is at the top of my bucket list, and we are focused on having experiences and creating memories while we are still young."

When reviewing your goal, you want to be reminded of *why* you have this goal. Plus, this gives your accountability partners more ammo to push you if you start falling behind. "You set the goal!" is a lot less powerful than "C'mon, man! Aren't you focused on experiential living this year? You won't be this young forever. Machu Picchu is at the top of your bucket list!"

If you're reading this and choose not to apply it, you're choosing to live under your potential. This structure will improve your chances of succeeding.

The Three Forms of Accountability

Accountability comes in three forms: personal, private, and public.

Personal accountability happens on an individual level. These are promises you make to yourself. They are intimate and not to be shared with anyone else. The benefit to this form of accountability is that you can get very detailed in your intention without becoming insecure that others will judge you.

Sometimes, a goal like "Lose 15lbs by my brother's wedding in July *because* I am scared of what my family will think of the weight I have gained" is not necessarily something you want other people to know. You don't have to declare your goals to your Instagram feed for them to be effective.

Private accountability happens in closed circles. My Success Buddies groups are examples of private accountability, since only a few people are aware of your goals. They are still intimate, but others can now support you on your mission and hold you accountable.

By allowing a group of people to get to know you on an intimate level, you can build trust. That trust will encourage you to share more openly about your goals, enabling your accountability partners to provide more profound feedback.

Public accountability happens in open circles. Posting a goal on your Instagram feed for the world to see is an example of public accountability because countless people are now aware of it. These are less intimate, but in the right situation, having a large number of people encouraging you can be very effective.

What happens when you stack all three forms of accountability together? Something magical. I like to call it All-Star Accountability. You keep the same goal but share different levels of intention. It might look something like this:

- Personal: Lose 15lbs by my brother's wedding in July *because* I fear what my family will think of the weight I have gained.
- Private: Lose 15lbs by my brother's wedding.
- Public: I'm excited to start going to the gym again. It's been years!

With All-Star Accountability, you're reviewing your personal intention daily, you're reviewing your private goal with your group, who will support you in achieving your desired weight, and you're letting the world know you're on a mission to be healthier. People might strike up conversations with you about the gym on social media, which will reinforce your new active identity.

When you leverage all three forms of accountability, I see nothing but a win-win-win situation.

Choosing Accountability Partners

If you're the smartest person in the room, you should find a new room.

Have you ever heard that saying?

There is some truth to it. As I have mentioned (a few times), I believe you are the average of the five people you spend the most time with. **If you're spending time with five millionaires, you'll be the sixth millionaire. If you hang out with five bums, you'll be the sixth bum.** I used to think I could manage negative relationships and they couldn't impact me, but that is not true. Having negative people in your inner circle will subtly drag you down.

Now, I look for the following criteria in people I surround myself with, which I call my Accountability Non-Negotiables:

- They are positive and grateful.
- They are actively working to become better at something.
- They have achieved what I want to achieve (or are aiming to).
- They are willing to give and receive constructive criticism.

That fourth characteristic is the most important to me. I want accountability partners who are not afraid to call me out when I am underperforming or to challenge my reasoning on major goals. Life is too short to be let off the hook when you're living under your potential.

If you haven't found people who fit the criteria mentioned above, try connecting with others in the comment section of your favorite personal development influencer. Social media is a great way to connect with like-minded people who have similar goals. A courteous approach could involve initiating a conversation regarding their latest book, course, or recent insightful post.

How to Structure Meetings

My meeting structure has changed quite a few times over the years, but here are some high-level, tried and tested rules to follow so that you can start building your own accountability group:

Frequency. I recommend meeting once per week. Find a weekly time slot that works for everyone in your group and send a recurring calendar invite. Since your activity trackers will be measuring goals on a weekly basis, that is also the frequency you should be meeting with your group.

Duration. I recommend 20 minutes per person. We call this a "hot seat." If your group has three members, meet for an hour. If it has six members, meet for two hours. After experimenting with different durations, 20 minutes seems to be the sweet spot where each member can recap their weekly goals and results, and other members can ask them questions.

Group Size. This is a tricky one. On one hand, the more accountability you can have in your life, the better. On the other, you don't want to be responsible for too many other people. Keeping up on the activity of a dozen other people would distract you from your own goals. I think somewhere between three and six group members is ideal.

Leadership. I recommend a rotating moderator. This means that each week, a different group member leads the discussion. It's the moderator who decides the order of the speakers, brings the conversation back on track if it strays, and wraps up each person's turn if they're approaching the 20-minute mark.

Content. During each 20-minute hot seat, the member who is speaking should start by reviewing their biggest goals from the previous week and the results of their effort. The moderator can then invite questions or suggestions from the rest of the group. After recapping, the moderator should give that member a chance to discuss their goals moving into the next week.

Praise vs. Criticism. Each member should try to balance both equally. **A great accountability partner feels just as happy when another member accomplishes their goals as they do when they accomplish their own.** Celebrate. Compliment. Congratulate. When another member fails, don't let it slide. You must provide constructive criticism and hold them accountable to the high standards they deserve. Treat each other how you want to be treated. There are no participation trophies here, only progress.

Great Feedback/Questions. Something I have noticed over the years is the difference between great feedback/questions and lazy feedback/questions. Laziness stems from a lack of commitment and can be poisonous to the health of your accountability group. A group member might say, "I have no feedback this week," or ask lazy questions like, "Will you do better next time?" In contrast, great questions challenge the member in the hot seat. After taking the time to review a member's activity tracker, a great question might sound like this: "I see you've failed to meet your reading goal for four weeks in a row now. Do you still think the goal is achievable? Do you really value it? Or should you reduce your goal to make it more attainable?" Do you see how that starts a conversation as opposed to ignoring the failure or allowing the hot seat member off the hook by answering with a simple "Yes"? Being a valuable group member means being a great listener, providing great feedback, and asking great questions.

Consequences. If a group member regularly skips meetings without a good explanation, fails to update their activity tracker, or doesn't seem to care about hitting their goals, you should fire them. Setting these expectations from the start will help you avoid hurting anyone's feelings. You're only as strong as your weakest link and if you tolerate mediocrity, your group will suffer.

Quarterly Checkups. Once per quarter, it's a good idea to zoom out and look at your life from a broader perspective, instead of a weekly perspective. During these meetings, moderators focus conversations on quarterly and yearly goals to make sure weekly goals are still aligned. It's always fascinating to see how fast and often our focus seems to change. These meetings act as realignment meetings, reminding you of what you should be focused on.

Yearly Reviews. At the end of each year, schedule in a longer meeting where each group member can reflect on their year and discuss their successes and failures at a more macro level. I like to prepare for these meetings by going back through my weekly activity tracker and journaling about my successes and failures. We usually overestimate how much we can do in a year and underestimate how much we can do in a week. I usually fail to hit my yearly goals because, although they are attainable, they are always very ambitious. I enjoy going back and finding ways to improve my odds for the next year. Progress is the name of the game.

Does anyone come to mind when you think about starting your own group? Send them a copy of this book and see what they think of this chapter!

Activity Tracker Template

The purpose of your activity tracker is two-fold:

- To track your weekly, monthly, quarterly, and yearly goals and results
- To provide visibility of your activity to your accountability partners

These trackers can be as simple or as complex as you want them to be. I have created a template you can access at https://tinyurl.com/riseofthereader. To have an editable version, you'll have to make a copy for yourself.

On the first tab, you will see a blank template. Hover over each of the fields to see a description of its intended purpose. On the second tab, you can see how a completed week would look with a bit more detail.

Activity Tracker Explained

As you're reading or listening to this next section, you might find it helpful to bring up the tracker on a laptop or tablet (rather than a phone screen), so that you can follow along as I explain each section. If you're not able to, feel free to come back to it later when you're building your own personalized tracker.

Google Sheets. Not only are Google Sheets free and easy to use, but they can be accessed from any device. Updating your activity from a mobile device is not always the easiest, but if you're in a hurry and updating on the fly, it can be a lifesaver. Google Sheets are sharable, giving your accountability partners real-time access to your data so that they can check in on your progress throughout the week and provide a push where necessary. My groups always manage our trackers in the same sheet but using separate tabs. This ensures everyone is using the same template and tracking activity in a similar way.

Daily Progress Section. As you can see, the main portion of the sheet is for tracking your daily progress. By tracking daily, you can identify hiccups, aka days of the week where you fail to execute. For people with a normal working schedule, hiccups tend to happen mostly on weekends. It also helps you keep track of what you have executed daily against what is left. Above this section, I have marked the week's start date for organizational purposes. This helps me go back in time should I ever need to review a specific week.

Groups and Activities. To the left of the Daily Progress Section, you'll see two columns labeled Groups and Activities. Groups are useful for stacking activities together into routines or for focusing on certain areas of your life. Examples of Groups in the template are Morning Routine and Health Goals. The Activities column is a place to describe the activity you'll be executing. Within the Morning Routine Group are activities like Wake Up at 6:30 a.m. and Make Morning Coffee.

Goal. To the right of the Daily Progress Section, you'll see three columns labeled Goal, Multiplier, and Net. The Goal column is where you list how many times you aim to achieve the desired activity during that week. In the Wake Up at 6:30 a.m. activity, you can see I have listed a Goal of five and blocked off Saturday and Sunday. This means that instead of a maximum of seven opportunities to achieve this goal, I have only given myself five.

Multiplier. In the Multiplier column you can make certain activities more valuable. This is useful for many reasons. First, not all activities are created equal. Let's say you're very focused on losing weight and the outcome of that goal will mean the world to you. If you miss a healthy eating goal, it should count as a bigger loss than missing some miscellaneous goal like flossing your teeth. This way, important activities count for more and less important activities carry less weight. The multiplier is not something we started with, but over time, it became a solution for the scenario above. If a group member is consistently missing a certain goal, you can recommend they multiply it so that it is worth more.

Net. Net allows you to quickly see what activities still need to be completed on a weekly basis and how many more times you must complete them to hit your target. I have set this column to show in red when there are outstanding goals and I am always trying my best to clear the read from my tracker.

Activity Completion Percentage. This field sits at the bottom of the Goal, Multiplier, and Net columns and allows you to measure your overall success from week to week. It also allows you to quickly review your accountability partners' sheets and see how they're doing from a zoomed-out perspective. Let's say you had a total of 100 Activity Points and you only completed 75. That would be a 75% completion rate. If your previous week was higher, let's say 85%, you could have a conversation with your group about why that is and what you can do better moving forward.

Week Streak. On the far right, you'll see the Week Streak column. While using a Fitbit to track my steps, I noticed that every time I hit my goal for a few days in a row, I was more likely to continue to achieve my step target in the days that followed. Why? Because I didn't want to break my streak.

It became a fun competition between me and my friends with Fitbits to see who could get the longest streak. This concept is often referred to as "gamification." We decided to apply the same thing to our activity trackers. Now, if you hit a goal for a handful of weeks in a row, you'll go out of your way to make sure you don't drop the ball. On the other hand, if you fail to hit a goal for multiple weeks in a row, the group can dig in during your hot seat session and ask what the deal is.

Monthly, Quarterly, and Yearly Goals. Below the Daily Progress Section, I keep track of my monthly, quarterly, and yearly goals. I try to handle this systematically. Each December/January, when I set my yearly goals, I break them down into quarterly goals. From there, I break them down into monthly goals and I also like to leave some room for changing priorities. This way, I always have my eyes on the bigger picture: I can make sure my weekly goals are aligned with my monthly goals, my monthly goals are aligned with my quarterly goals, and my quarterly goals are aligned with my yearly goals. Most importantly, I can make sure my yearly goals are aligned with who I want to be as a person and the overall life I want to be living.

Comparison Creates Joy

"Comparison is the thief of joy" is one of those common phrases you'll hear in life. Although it has some merit when it comes to social media or lifestyle choice, I have a bone to pick with it regarding personal development and accountability.

I believe that when leveraged correctly, comparison creates joy.

Comparison is the best tool available for measuring your individual life progress. It's only by comparing your present circumstances to your past circumstances that you can see how far you've come. Without measurement, there can be no progress.

For example, whenever I am feeling down or having a bad day, I simply compare my present to my past, and I am instantly relieved of the bad feelings. It is all about comparing yourself to yourself, not others. Comparison creates gratitude. Comparison creates clarity. Comparison creates joy.

On the macro level, remember that no matter what you're going through, someone always has it worse than you. If you have food on the table and a roof over your head, you're fortunate. Use comparison as a tool for good instead of allowing it to tear you down.

This perspective shift has done wonders for my mental health.

The Path of Most Resistance

It's our natural human response to always look for the path of least resistance.

This is our default because until the last couple of hundred years, conserving energy and resources was imperative for survival. Food and water were universally scarce and at any moment, you could be attacked by a wild animal. In those times, it was important to have as much energy in reserve as possible.

Although our circumstances have changed, our brains have not. At a neurological level, we are still programmed to take the path of least resistance, which is why so many people have a hard time getting up and going to work. I am here to say we are all capable of doing more and we should find accountability partners who remind us of that.

I encourage everyone reading this book to **take the path of most resistance**.

Have you heard about the relationship between value and pain? It's fascinating. **The more valuable something is, the more pain you must**

be prepared to face to achieve it. In economics, it's called supply and demand. The most valuable positions in life, like having a great relationship, a prestigious career, or a stress-free lifestyle, all require a lot of hard work. If these things were easy to come by, they would not be deemed valuable anymore.

This is why we are not all magically walking around in perfect relationships with six-pack abs and living in beachfront mansions. These things are reserved for people willing to take the path of most resistance and endure the pain of discipline for years. The higher the mountain, the more you must climb. The taller the tree, the taller the shadow.

Think about a game like chess. If you were able to simply move the pieces around freely and there were no rules, it wouldn't be any fun. The value that playing chess provides comes from its difficulty. The rules of the game are harsh but rewarding. The same is true for life.

The most fulfillment is going to come from the road less traveled. Since we are programmed to default to the other path, the easier path most people follow, we need accountability. We need people in our corner, ready to remind us of what we can become. People who can grab us as we start defaulting to our comfort zones and show us where true value lives. Find those people and encourage them to be strict with you.

9. Implementing What You Learn

I recently found myself talking with Sharon Lechter.

Sharon is the co-author of *Rich Dad Poor Dad*, the book that started my passion for reading. The moment was surreal to me because it showed that my reading journey had really come full circle.

One moment I am opening my first personal development book and just a few years later, I am telling the full origin story of my journey to the fabulous woman who wrote the book. What happened next was unexpected.

After I finished telling my story and thanked Sharon, she replied, "Don't thank me. Thank yourself."

Confused, I asked, "What do you mean?"

Sharon answered, "Nick, do you know that over 32 million copies of that book have been sold? I can only imagine how many times each copy has been passed around." At that moment, I realized that my original copy had been read by at least five different people.

She continued, **"Out of the countless people who have read that book, only a small portion used the information on those pages to truly transform their lives. So, instead of thanking me, I would encourage you to pat yourself on the back. You are the one who created change."**

The lesson? Simply reading these books will not change your life. You must implement them to create a real difference.

Said another way: **You can read every book that has ever been written about push-ups, but if you never get down on the ground and do them, you won't grow muscle. No one else can do your push-ups for you.**

The Rising Reader's Book Implementation Framework

Looking back, implementation came naturally to me because of those early days during my college internship and my job selling software after graduation. When I sold a software package to a new customer, it would always include a phase called "implementation."

During implementation, new customers would have to attend training sessions, study what they learned, and practice using the software before their next session. This framework was based on hundreds of successful implementations. If a customer did not follow our instructions, they would usually fail to get up and running on the software. This phase could last anywhere from six to 18 weeks, depending on the size of the company.

I found that I naturally applied a similar approach to the books I was reading. **Instead of just reading the books, I would study my notes and practice what I had learned. I felt like a human guinea pig, testing the tips and strategies I was learning on myself.** Otherwise, I thought, I would be just like the companies that didn't take their software implementation seriously and end up wasting time and money.

Here is a high-level overview of my Rising Reader's Book Implementation Framework:

- Step 1: Set an Intention
- Step 2: Find the Best Books
- Step 3: Schedule Reading Time
- Step 4: Take Effective Notes
- Step 5: Find Lead Measures
- Step 6: Add to Activity Tracker
- Step 7: Execute and Measure
- Step 8: Celebrate Small Wins
- Step 9: Decide Next Steps
- Step 10: Share the Results
- Step 11: Review Book Notes

Let's expand on each of these steps so that you can try them for yourself.

Step 1: Set an Intention

As we discussed at the outset, you want to start with each book by identifying an area for improvement and defining your intentions. You will be reviewing this intention each time you open the book, so make sure it is something you truly desire. Once you have this figured out, you're on your way to becoming a Rising Reader.

Example: A few years ago, I found myself getting sleepy toward the end of my workdays. At college, it seemed like I had infinite energy, but I was starting to notice signs of fatigue. Was I just getting old? This was an area for improvement. After talking through the problem with some friends, they suggested I work on improving my sleep. Using the goal-setting framework from the previous chapter, I set my goal to be "Find at least three ways to improve my sleep and implement them in the next 30 days, *because* I am tired of crashing in the early afternoon, and I want to get more out of my day."

Step 2: Find the Best Books

By surveying your friends and mentors or doing some online research, you can find the best book(s) available for achieving your goal.

Example: When those friends suggested I try to improve my sleep, I asked if they had any book recommendations. Unfortunately, they didn't. So, like most things in life, I Googled it. After I found a few book titles of interest, I went over to Amazon to read some reviews. I decided to start by reading *Why We Sleep* by Dr. Matthew Walker. Plus, I saw that he was interviewed on The Joe Rogan Experience, one of my favorite podcasts. If Joe liked what he had to say, I bet I would too.

Step 3: Schedule Reading Time

Scheduling reading time into your calendar is one of the most important parts of the reading process. In Chapter 5, you might recall how quickly 15 minutes of reading when you wake up in the morning and another 15 minutes before bed can change your life. Those are the times of day where distractions are naturally limited, and you can focus on the book.

Example: In my case, I already had daily reading blocks scheduled in my calendar. Once a new book arrives and I finish the book I'm reading, I don't 'take a break,' I continue with my momentum. Sticking to your schedule is important. Remember, it's not the consequences of missing one day of reading that hurts; it's losing your momentum and having to start up again that does the damage. This small step in the right direction, repeated over a long period of time, will lead to huge rewards. Don't mess it up!

Step 4: Take Effective Notes

Chapter 5 was dedicated to taking effective notes while reading. If you skipped over that section or failed to take effective notes while reading it, please go back and review. **Without rockstar notes, you will not achieve rockstar results**.

Example: As I was reading *Why We Sleep*, I continued to take notes on anything that might help improve my sleep or my energy. I remember this book was full of useful information. Once finished, I grouped my notes into categories like Action Items, General Notes, Quotes, More Research Required, Further Reading, or Miscellaneous. This led me right into the next step.

Step 5: Find Lead Measures

Here, you want to review your notes and identify lead measures to help you achieve your goal. Lead measures are the actions that I can implement to improve my sleep that will directly influence the outcome—they are directly influenceable by me. The outcome I was aiming for was better sleep, which we call a "lag measure."

Example: Some of the lead measures I noted while reading included actions like installing room-darkening curtains in my bedroom, wearing an eye mask while I slept, having a more consistent wakeup time, and not snacking after dinner, among other things. See how those items are measures (actions) that will lead to my desired outcome of more sleep? Now that we have them selected, we can begin the fun part.

Step 6: Add to Activity Tracker

We thoroughly covered activity trackers and how to use them in Chapter 8. Now, by adding your lead measures into your spreadsheet and reviewing them, you'll be able to manage progress. Measurement is key.

Example: I decided to take each of the activities from Step 5 and put them into my spreadsheet. For a one-time activity like installing blackout curtains, I had a goal of one. Once it was done, it was done. For other activities that will happen on a more regular basis, you can set bigger goals and keep them from week to week. For the other three items on the sheet, I set a weekly goal of five days out of seven. That way, I could ease myself into the new activity and leave some flexibility for the weekend.

You can see a basic version of what this looked like here:

Activity Name	M	T	W	T	F	S	S	Goal
Install Blackout Curtains in Bedroom								1
Start Wearing Blackout Eye Mask While Sleeping								5
No Food After Dinner								5
Wake up at 8:00AM								5

Step 7: Execute and Measure

Start executing. At this point, you have identified a problem, stated your intention, found a good book, scheduled reading time, read your book, taken great notes, identified important lead measures, and put them into your spreadsheet. You are in now a great position to go through your week and measure your activity. **Each of these steps was preparing you for execution.**

Example: As you can see below, during the first week, I was able to successfully implement some of these activities, but not all of them. During the beginning of the week, I hit all my activities, but by the time Thursday rolled around, I fell off the wagon. There is no shame in coming up short. You can use that as motivation to try again next week and talk with your accountability buddies about why you failed and what you can do to improve your chances of success during the next week.

Activity Name	M	T	W	T	F	S	S	Goal
Install Blackout Curtains in Bedroom				x				1
Start Wearing Blackout Eye Mask While Sleeping	x	x	x	x	x			5
No Food After Dinner	x	x	x		x			5
Wake up at 8:00AM	x	x	x		x			5

Step 8: Celebrate Small Wins

Often, implementing a new activity is challenging. To combat this, and to stay motivated, it's important to celebrate small wins and to show gratitude daily. I try to do both things as I complete each activity or in the morning when I'm reviewing that day's activity. If you see me in a coffee shop patting myself on the back or throwing my hands up in the air like I just scored a touchdown in the Super Bowl, I am celebrating my small wins.

Example: As I completed the activities listed above, I celebrated each one with a little pat on the back and a show of gratitude. It probably sounded like this, "Congratulations, Nick, for waking up today on time. Remember, you're doing this *because* you want to have more energy throughout the workday. I am grateful for my bed and my ability to wake up healthy, wealthy, and happy." If you keep stacking wins and celebrating them, each activity will get easier and easier as time goes on.

Step 9: Decide Next Steps

Once you're a few weeks into your new habit, you should pause to take stock and see if it's working. You don't want to implement something inconvenient in the hope that it will help you only to find yourself still doing it years later with no results. The ability to quantify different improvements in your health, wealth, or happiness can be hard to measure, but do your best. The good news is that nowadays, there are devices to measure most health-related goals and financial tools to measure most wealth-related ones. For happiness, I have found journaling to be the best measurement tool. If the lead measure (activity) gets you closer to your goal, keep it. If it doesn't, drop it and try to find a more beneficial activity. Life is too short to hold on to bad habits.

Example: For my goal of getting better sleep, I decided to measure my progress by wearing an Oura Ring, a wearable sleep tracker that provides data on a dozen different sleep-related metrics. After establishing a baseline for my total sleep, time in bed, sleep efficiency, and resting heart rate, I could confidently see if I was able to improve these variables after implementing the activities above. Thankfully, I did. The results were amazing. By improving my sleep, I was able to eliminate my afternoon fatigue and get more done at work. I decided to keep all those improvements and I still manage them to this day.

Step 10: Share the Results

Share your results with others who have similar goals. By sharing your journey, you help to improve the lives of others around you too. Not only are you contributing to the common good, but you're also helping to compound your own progress. Teaching others helps you retain the information you're learning so that it's readily available in your brain whenever you need it. Since you are the average of the five people you spend the most time with, if their lives are improving, so is yours. Be the one who drives that average sky-high.

Example: After making dramatic improvements to my sleep and eliminating my daytime sleepiness, I knew I had to share this recipe with everyone around me. However, I have learned over the years not to push personal development information on people who aren't looking for it, so I had to be careful. Even today, I always start by asking for permission when wanting to give someone advice. It might sound like, "Hey, coworker! I recently made some changes to my sleep routine and naturally added an incredible amount of energy to my afternoon. I see you've been yawning a lot lately and having some afternoon espressos. Are you open to hearing about what I've implemented for myself?" I have had this conversation dozens of times. Sometimes, I wonder how many late afternoon coffees I have stolen away from Starbucks… (Haha!)

Step 11: Review Book Notes

Finally, make sure to revisit your book notes regularly for more opportunities to learn. It would shock you how many times I have reviewed my notes from an old book and found something I missed the first or second time through. Sometimes, I find useful information for totally unrelated topics. Remember Book Sex? When two random book ideas come together and create something original and fun (aka a Book Baby)? It's the best.

Example: When your sleep dramatically improves and your new habits become normal, you might fall into a state of complacency. By reviewing your notes and refreshing yourself on how far you have come, you can maintain your attitude of gratitude. I often take concepts from the book that I was not able to apply when I read it and work them into solutions for different areas of my life.

Stop and Implement or Start Another Book?

As with many areas of personal development reading, there are no "right" answers, but I would like to share my perspective on this topic since I am often asked about it.

Reading books and implementing the information you learn from them are two separate activities, and they should be treated as such.

Rising Readers schedule daily reading time into their calendars, and I believe that schedule should remain there, even when life is busy or distracting. You do not want to lose the momentum you have. Remember, small steps in the right direction over a long period of time will lead to disproportionately positive results. You don't stop brushing your teeth every day if you decide to start flossing, right? You keep brushing your teeth while adding the flossing into your morning hygiene routine.

Eliminating bad habits and implementing better ones can be as simple as starting a flossing routine or as complex as changing professions. It's your responsibility to make it work.

When people tell me I am reading too much, I like to tell them I only read for an hour or two a day, whereas I spend every other waking moment implementing what I have read.

Although I am not literally focused on implementing what I have read for 15 hours a day, it does feel like it sometimes and that is not a bad thing. **Life is a game, and you might as well win at it.**

Implementing Too Much

Is there a point where you can implement too much from a book?

I go back and forth between implementing as much as I can and being as selective as I can.

If your intention is clear, why not push your limits? There are times when I add 10 new activities to my activity tracker in a single week. **Oftentimes, I find that my preconceived notion of what is possible is only limited by my thinking and that I can fly right past that limit with ease.**

The world is like an infinite buffet, offering endless options for us on which to spend our time and energy. Instead of asking God for lighter burdens, you can ask for stronger shoulders. One of the quickest ways to kill your momentum is by putting artificial limits on your capabilities.

Other times, I overestimate my bandwidth and find myself spread too thin. I reach a point of diminishing returns when implementing too many new behaviors hurts the results. I think of myself as a book note hoarder when this happens, trying to save too many things from each book.

In these moments, being selective and choosing the 20% of activities that will lead to 80% of the results is usually better.

I would encourage you to do as I do and flirt the line between just enough and too much. This is the point where you can grow the most and where a little bit of failure is just part of the process.

Progress happens when you're pushing these boundaries.

Failing to Implement

As I mentioned before, failing to implement something from a book you've just finished is common. Many of the things we read about are elaborate and take time to absorb. I have failed to keep up with a new habit many times, but I never get discouraged. Why? Because I know I am always making progress.

Step 8 of The Rising Reader's Book Implementation Framework asks us to celebrate small wins and show gratitude daily. For instance, if I was looking to improve my sleep by installing a more consistent wakeup time and I accidentally slept in, I would keep my internal dialogue as positive as I can. "You did an amazing job sticking to this new wakeup time up until today. Today's failure is nothing but an opportunity to learn. I am grateful for this challenge, and I look forward to starting a new win streak tomorrow morning."

By implementing an activity tracker and meeting with your accountability buddies, you can bring up your failure as a point of discussion. Additional perspective from group members can be very useful. If you continue missing an activity, asking for additional accountability such as daily check-ins can help. Recently, one of my buddies needed help waking up on time. I offered to call him each morning and ensure he was out of bed and starting his morning routine until he felt comfortable with this change and could confidently manage it himself.

We are all imperfect humans. If you're effortlessly installing new behaviors without failure, you might not be challenging yourself enough. Flirt that line, otherwise, you're leaving some progress on the table and you will come to regret it.

PART III:
Conclusion

10. Delayed Gratification

Early in my personal development journey, I stumbled upon a quote from Jerry Rice: **"Today I will do what others won't, so tomorrow I will do what others can't."**[17]

Instantly, I started visualizing myself working my butt off over the coming years to retire by 35. That's the dream, right? Work hard and work smart when you're young so that you can reap the rewards before that whole "wealth in a wheelchair" thing that happens to most people.

For the next couple of years, I did just that. I started wearing my long working hours as a badge of honor and casually said things like, "Oh, you worked 40 hours this week? I remember my first part-time job." I really did put in 60- to 80-hour weeks for a couple of years in a row, including the time I spent studying and implementing personal development material.

In a world of instant gratification, it felt great to outwork many of my friends. The more I worked, the faster everything seemed to be coming to fruition. My financial position improved, but so did my value to the company I was working for and just about everything else in my personal life.

The Stanford Marshmallow Experiment

The following study had a big impact on me and taught me the importance of delaying my gratification. It went like this:

In 1972, a group of researchers at Stanford University led by psychologist Walter Mischel hosted a study on delayed gratification. During the experiment, children were given a choice between a small immediate reward (one marshmallow or one pretzel stick), or two small rewards (two marshmallows or two pretzel sticks) if they waited for a period of time. The researchers then left the room for about 15 minutes. Upon their return, they offered rewards to the children who waited.

The researchers kept tabs on the children who participated in their study as they grew up and found that those who were able to wait for the additional reward tended to have more success as adults. They measured success with variables like SAT scores, educational attainment, body mass index, and more.

Follow-up studies continued to show a correlation between delaying gratification and life success.

Can you believe that? Children who can wait an extra 15 minutes for one extra marshmallow (or pretzel stick) will go on to lead more successful lives. Where does this come from and how can we install that programming for ourselves?

Be Kind to Your Future Self

Fighting against instant gratification is never easy.

When you combine a world where temptation sits at every corner with a brain that constantly craves its next hit of dopamine, you get an instant gratification society.

Back in Chapter 5, I mentioned a question you can ask when facing a difficult decision: "When I look back on this decision tomorrow, which option will leave me feeling more fulfilled?"

Imagine you're four miles into a five-mile run, you're feeling fatigued, and your brain starts doing what it always does—looking for a way out. Your self-talk switches from "You've got this, you running rock star!" to "Just quit now and try again next week. You're tired and all that pain will go away if you just stop running. It's cold outside and you have that leftover pizza you can heat up. Just quit now." With every step you take, the voice in your head gets louder and more convincing.

In situations like this, ask yourself the question above. If you stop running short of your goal, would you be fulfilled tomorrow when you think back on your run? Really try to put yourself in the future and reflect on what decision will lead to more fulfillment.

This line of thinking helps you minimize short-term destructive behavior and maximize long-term helpful behavior. I wish I knew this framework in college.

When I think about a world full of temptation, there is nothing that comes to mind faster than my college experience. Instead of studying for a test, I would often default to something more exciting like the dining hall, the gym, the bar, or Netflix. I would give in to my short-term need for dopamine and ignore my long-term need to ace the upcoming test.

Had I just asked myself that one focusing question, I could have avoided many last-minute study sessions and poor grades. Thankfully, even with my dopamine-seeking brain, I was still able to pass most of my college classes. Cs earn degrees, right, Mom? (Inside joke!)

Another useful tactic for delaying gratification and acting in your best interest is being empathetic and kind to your future self. When I was in the middle of those last-minute study sessions, I would always wonder why my past self hadn't been more aware of my future self. How could I have been so oblivious?

Stop hurting your future self!

This happens a lot with food—it certainly happened to me. You're hungry so you default to something mouth-watering and indulgent instead of something healthy and beneficial. In the short-term, you're happy. Moments later, though, your future self is cursing you. Bloated, a pound heavier, and inflamed. You wonder why your past self was so cruel.

Keep your future self front of mind and start guiding more of your decision-making through their lens.

Delayed Gratification in My Routines

Many of the activities in my morning and evening routines serve my future self more than my present self. It sounds funny, but I know my future self will thank me.

What does that mean exactly? Well, I think a lot about my future self. **There is the version of you tomorrow who will judge your actions from today, but there is also the version of you 20 years from now who will judge all your actions from this day forward.**

Be kind to all your future selves.

Activities such as meditation have some short-term benefits, but most of them come after years of practice and won't be realized until far into the future. When I first started meditating, I found it boring and didn't see how it could improve my life in the short-term. However, before giving up, I researched the subject a bit more, and found the following long-term benefits:

- Increased self-awareness
- Increased emotional intelligence
- Increased imagination and creativity
- Increased patience and tolerance
- Reduction of negative emotions
- Prevention of age-related memory loss
- Lengthened attention span

I am just over six years into my meditation journey, and I have already started to see changes in most of these categories. I can only imagine where I will be with them in 20 or 40 years… You're welcome, future self!

The painkiller vs. vitamin metaphor is a great way to think about this. Marketing and sales teams are always looking to promote and sell products or services that immediately reduce the pain their customers experience. Why? Because they are easier to sell. Since vitamins have no noticeable immediate effect after you take them, they are much harder to sell to people. As a consumer, I can understand this. If the benefits cannot be felt immediately and the future ROI is hard to measure, why should I spend my money?

Funny enough, vitamins are a great example of something I consume daily that my future self will thank me for. **I spend somewhere around $10 a day on vitamins, minerals, and other supplements. Why? So I can actively attend my grandkids' T-ball games and hike Machu Picchu again when I am 80 years old. I would rather feel 60 when I am 80 than 80 when I am 60.**

Vitamins, minerals, and other supplements are shown to reduce the chances of many major degenerative diseases.[18] **Prevention isn't sexy, but it is worth it.** Why waste all my time and squander my health now, only to be rich but unhealthy later? Then I would have to use my wealth just to stay alive. That is no fun. Better safe than sorry, especially when there are no downsides to an activity like taking vitamins.

The 80/20 Rule for Living Life to the Fullest

There is a fine line between living for today and living for tomorrow.

Are you familiar with the 80/20 Rule? It goes by other names, including The Pareto Principle, The Law of the Vital Few, or The Principle of Factor Sparsity.[19] Back in 1906, economist Vilfredo Pareto found that 80% of the land and wealth in Italy was owned by 20% of the population. After surveying several other countries, he found the same applied abroad.

This same ratio exists in many areas of our personal and professional lives. For me, I found that about 20% of my life experiences were leading to 80% of my overall happiness and fulfillment. I call these "highly leveraged activities."

That means that on the flipside, roughly 80% of my life experiences were leading to only 20% of my overall happiness and fulfillment. I call these "poorly leveraged activities."

My goal? Double, triple, or quadruple my time in highly leveraged activities and automate, delegate, or eliminate the time I spend in poorly leveraged activities. I achieved this using the frameworks I described in earlier chapters on eliminating unhealthy habits and installing healthy ones.

With my extra time, I was able to start servicing my future self. **I call this working *on* your life instead of working *in* your life.**

After going through a few cycles of this process, I found that many of the activities leading to the most short-term happiness and fulfillment also led to a lot of long-term happiness and fulfillment. Examples include reading personal development books and traveling the world.

With reading personal development books, I could educate myself in real-time and act on what I was learning. Not only was this exciting for me in the short-term, but future Nick was always singing my praises because I was helping him too. With world travel, I can feed all my core values during the experience, while also giving my future self some cherished memories to relive. Author Bill Perkins calls these 'memory dividends' in his book, *Die With Zero*.

When you experience something amazing and you document it well, you can collect dividends from that experience each time you relive it. These memory dividends work just like financial dividends. You invest once and get paid out forever. Take a moment to think back to your favorite travel experience. It could be a trip to your local movie theater with your family or an extravagant safari in South Africa. Whatever it is, close your eyes and let it consume for a while.

That warm and fuzzy feeling is a memory dividend. You're experiencing happiness and fulfillment by reliving something that happened to you in the past. How wonderful is that? **Your past self had fun and your future self can access it whenever they like through storytelling, photos and videos, or visualization.**

Two birds with one stone, as they say.

If you're trying to live a more exciting life, I recommend living as though millions of people are watching you on TV. If your life is boring and your energy low, those people are going to change the channel. Conversely, if you constantly put yourself in stimulating and interesting situations, people will stay tuned in. The process is perpetuated if you consistently seek adventure and steer clear of a dull, sedentary life. Pretend people are watching over your shoulder, and things will get more interesting.

Another way to think about this is to pretend that after you die, you'll be forced to watch your life replayed like a movie, repeatedly. You don't want to bore your future self, do you?

So, what is the ideal balance between tending to your current self and your future self? Totally up to you. For me, it is probably 80/20—that magic ratio again. I spend 80% of my time on highly leveraged present-moment experiences and 20% on being kind to my future self. The best part is that most of my highly leveraged present-moment experiences are also feeding my future self.

Learning to Love the Process

It's a cliché, but most of the time, the real pleasure really is in the process.

You've probably seen some version of this statement a hundred times—on bumper stickers, in Instagram posts, and on those little feel-good signs at restaurants or boutiques. We take sayings like this for granted because we see them so often. Clichés are clichés for a reason, after all. I try to stop and analyze them whenever they pop up instead of letting them in one ear and out the other.

With this one, it took me a while to truly understand it. Let's stay on the subject of travel. Many people find that they enjoy the anticipation of travel more than the experience itself. The rush of buying plane tickets and selecting hotels or Airbnb is amazing. Researching destinations and booking fun excursions is one of my favorite parts of the process. Telling coworkers, friends, and family about the exciting things you're going to do brings a smile to your face. The happiness you feel while visualizing your experience is half the fun.

There is nothing wrong with this. In fact, it can be very useful.

Entrepreneur Gary Vaynerchuk's story is one of my favorite examples of this. As a young immigrant kid with an accent, Gary wanted to fit in with his fellow classmates. Since everyone around him loved the New York Jets, his local NFL football team, Gary quickly became a fan as well. That was his way of fitting in and helped him gain confidence around new people.

These days, Gary is extremely successful. He tells people he works so hard so that he can live out his childhood dream of buying the franchise. Yes, literally buying the New York Jets. The interesting part is that you'll sometimes catch Gary admitting that he hopes he never gets to buy the team because he is motivated by the chase. He says he has fallen in love with the process, not the outcome. His joy comes from pursuing the goal of buying the team instead of the act of buying it.

They say that the man who loves walking will walk farther than the man who loves the destination. I have found the same thing in my life. I love what I do daily, and I am motivated by living out my process. Yes, I dream of big things, but I do not allow my happiness to depend on achieving them. Achieving my biggest goals is more like a bonus to me, not the actual reward. I truly do enjoy the passage of time.

One final thought on this subject: learn how to love the boring and challenging stuff too. As long as that work is highly leveraged, of course. It takes a special type of discipline to sit down and work on a project like this book. It was much harder than I initially anticipated. I know, though, that at the end of the day, my future self will be so happy I willed this book into existence. The same goes for activities like running. I find running very boring, but I know my future self will thank me. **By thinking about my future self, I can be mindful of and enjoy the process.**

As they say, suffer the pain of discipline or suffer the pain of regret. The part they forget to mention is that the pain of discipline is temporary, and the pain of regret lasts forever.

11. Paradigm Shifts

Have you ever had an "Aha!" moment?

When it happens, something in your life is instantly transformed from unclear to clear. You take off a pair of blurry glasses and replace them with a pair that allows you to truly see a situation clearly for the first time.

Well, throughout my reading journey, I have upgraded the lens through which I see the world many times. I am constantly searching for new world views—new lenses—that allow me to become healthier, wealthier, and happier.

These are not simply mindset shifts. These are paradigm shifts.

As we grow up, our parents, our communities, our classrooms, and our media shape the way we see the world and condition us to see it through a unique set of lenses, whereas our mindsets can shift from moment to moment. It takes far more work to bring about a change to these deeply programmed paradigms.

The beauty of a paradigm shift, though, is that once you've upgraded the lens through which you view the world and thrown away your old views, it is hard to go back.

Major Life Upgrades

The Victim to Hero Upgrade

In the first book I read on my journey, *Rich Dad Poor Dad*, the authors taught me to shift my default response from something limiting to something challenging, from "I can't" to "How can I?" In other words, shifting from victim to hero. Instead of running from a challenge, analyze it and find a way to conquer it.

- "I can't run a marathon," becomes "How can I run a marathon?"
- "I can't afford that car," becomes "How can I afford that car?"
- "I can't be happy like that person," becomes "How can I be happy like that person?"

I am now the hero of my own story, and it feels amazing. With this upgraded lens, I am more optimistic about the challenges I face. My brain is no longer fearful of those challenges and enjoys breaking them down so I can make progress. When I am presented with a big challenge, I ask myself this question: How do you eat an elephant? The answer? One bite at a time.

The 'You Can Learn from Everyone' Upgrade

Unfortunately, the world today is quite divisive. Political, social, and religious views have created enemies out of neighbors and cause fights in every corner of the internet. For what? One of the biggest concepts to impact me over the last couple of years is the realization that we are all just people and most of us want the same things in life. There are 8 billion people on our planet and each of them has a unique world view.

Instead of tuning someone out because their views differ from your own, realize that you have something to learn from them. Walk a mile in their shoes and maybe you'd carry the same beliefs you currently find unattractive. I seek out authors who have totally different views from my own so that I can diversify my own perspective and have more empathy for people I don't understand.

If your neighbor has a different opinion than you on a major social issue, hear them out. Sit down, remain calm, and ask good questions. You'll be surprised what you can learn from that person. **For the rest of my life, I am choosing never to shut someone out or refuse to converse with them because they have a different opinion than me.**

The Astronaut Upgrade

Have you ever looked at photos of Earth taken from space? If not, you should stop right now and search for one—they are amazing. The incredible part is that in these pictures, you can cover the whole planet with your thumb. Gone. Our wondrous planet is a mere dot in an infinite sea of other planets and stars. If you remove Earth, nothing changes. Our planet is full of wonderful people, architecture, works of art, ideas, and emotion. If all of that disappeared, almost nothing would change in the grand scheme of things.

What does this show me? It shows me not to sweat the small stuff. Life is too short, and our planet, in this vast universe, is too small for us to allow the most trivial of inconveniences to throw off our entire day.

To be reading this, your grandparents had to meet each other...and their grandparents before them. Can you believe how wild that is? **Take advantage of this opportunity you've been given to live a fruitful life and do something positive with it.** Living with this type of mentality and perspective allows me to stay positive and in control of my emotions in situations that used to easily throw me off.

The *Amor Fati* Upgrade

Throughout the last few years, I have found a lot of value in studying Stoic philosophy. At a high level, Stoicism teaches the values of self-control, logic, and courage as means of overcoming damaging emotions.

It teaches us to differentiate between the things within our control and those that are not. We have control over our thoughts and our reactions to external stimuli. We do not have control over external events, such as other people's actions, or worldly events, like weather or our inevitable death. Therefore, to achieve inner peace, we should focus on the things within our control and not let those outside our control put us into a negative headspace.

The philosopher Nietzsche took this teaching to the next level with the Latin phrase *amor fati*[20]. It translates to "love of one's fate," meaning everything that happens outside your sphere, including suffering and loss, should be viewed as good or necessary. **You have a choice to view everything in life the way that benefits you the most.**

Life happens. **By releasing the need to control everything and shifting into a headspace of indifference for the things outside our control, we are less susceptible to negative thinking.** This has led to a more consistent lifestyle for me and has given me the opportunity to focus on gratitude in situations that would have thrown me off in years past.

The *Memento Mori* Upgrade

Memento mori, as we now know, is Latin phrase meaning "Remember you must die." At first glance, this seems dark and chilling, but as we talked about it earlier in the book, it can be very positive. Too many of us overestimate the amount of time we have left on this beautiful planet. As a result, we procrastinate and constantly push our dreams off until tomorrow. We end up regretting the time we waste on poorly leveraged activities.

By constantly reminding ourselves we have a limited amount of time to chase our dreams, we can prioritize our time more efficiently and take less of it for granted. I mentioned this earlier in the book, but I have the phrase *Memento mori* tattooed on my chest, right above my heart. Whenever I am feeling lazy or unproductive, I simply look in the mirror and focus on the heart beating below the tattoo. It won't beat forever. We are mortal.

Don't fall prey to the idea that you have infinite time on this planet. Seneca reminds us of this in his book, *On the Shortness of Life,* where he says, **"It is not that we have so little time but that we lose so much. ... The life we receive is not short, but we make it so; we are not ill-provided but use what we have wastefully."**[21] Start focusing on this and let the magic of mortality guide your actions.

The Planting a Tree Upgrade

If you're struggling with urgency and *memento mori* is not your thing, try this upgrade. It stems from my favorite Chinese proverb, **"The best time to plant a tree was 20 years ago. The second-best time is now."**

I believe we can all design the life we want to live while making a positive impact on everyone around us in the process. That takes effort and discipline. Remember, you can either suffer the pain of discipline or the pain of regret. **The pain of discipline weighs a lot less than the pain of regret.**

The more valuable something is to you, the more pain you're going to have to experience to achieve it. By starting today and allowing your actions to compound, you're going to reach your dreams a lot faster than if you allow yourself to wait to start tomorrow. I have kept this quote on the

RISE OF THE READER

background of my phone for a long time and review it whenever I am feeling a lack of motivation. It works wonders.

The Impact Upgrade

This upgrade states that your income depends on the number of people you're positively impacting. I owe this paradigm shift in myself to two books: *The Go-Giver* by Bob Burg and John David Mann and *The Millionaire Fastlane* by MJ DeMarco.

Think about the richest people you know. Simply put, they have the biggest positive impact on the most people. Large organizations like Amazon, Apple, and Walmart serve hundreds of millions of people each year. **The more people you can impact, the more you can earn.** How can you start positively impacting more people in your life? Does the role you currently play have the potential to grow? If not, is it time for a change?

There is a reciprocal relationship between giving and receiving here. The more you positively impact people, the more you're rewarded, in every way imaginable. What a great incentive. The more you're rewarded, the more you're able to improve your product or service so that it can positively impact even more people.

The Comfort Zone Upgrade

For much of my life, I stayed in my comfort zone and avoided discomfort. Why? It was easy. Feeling fear is not something humans naturally enjoy. Plus, I was full of insecurities and feared the judgment of others. Everything changed, however, when I heard a friend say, "Everything you want is just outside your comfort zone."

130

I realized I couldn't possibly live up to my potential if I never venture to the borders of my comfort zone. If everyone who ever achieved something of significance intentionally embraced discomfort, why shouldn't I try it? So, I started experimenting with fear. When your heart starts beating faster and you get a pit in your stomach, you know you're about to grow.

Now, I intentionally look for things that make me uncomfortable and I gravitate toward them. Author Kristen Butler, in her book *The Comfort Zone,* reminds us that venturing excessively beyond our comfort zone can lead to burnout and failure. I've discovered that embracing the edge between comfort and discomfort is where I experience the most personal growth – a gradual approach tends to yield the best results.

Adopting this character trait has enabled me to travel solo internationally, start businesses, speak on stages, and interview business celebrities. The old version of me, the one who lived deep inside his comfort zone, wouldn't believe who I have become. It didn't happen overnight. It was a slow, steady fight. I have dealt with hundreds of pits in my stomach and thoughts of retreat, but I knew I could become familiar with anything and rewire my brain to love and embrace fear. It can work for you too.

The Limitless Upgrade

This paradigm shifted for me when I read psychologist Carol Dweck's research on fixed vs. growth mindsets. Someone with a fixed mindset believes that intelligence, talent, and other qualities are things you're born with and are unchangeable. In contrast, someone with a growth mindset believes that intelligence and talent can be developed with practice and effort.

Growing up, I had a fixed mindset in just about every area of my life. I embraced my limits and allowed that false narrative to control me. Now,

I believe we are all limitless. We can change our brains and our realities. Remember, reality is negotiable.

There is a book about almost every subject known to man. If you want to start a business, learn an instrument, or change your profession, you can do it. Become a student of the world. By being intentional, studying the right material, and implementing what we learn, there are no limits to our potential. Believe this and you can achieve anything your heart desires.

Transition

These paradigm shifts changed my life, but so have other much smaller shifts in my daily habits and routines. The second half of this book is designed to highlight some of the smaller changes I have made and introduce you to a wide variety of subjects, books, and tools. Now that you've learned how to effectively read and implement these resources, you'll have an easier time adopting what you're interested in.

You don't have to read this next section straight through. Feel free to apply what you've learned from the first half and come back to these habits any time you're looking for additional subjects to explore.

Please STOP and share this book!

If you're enjoying this book and finding value in what you're learning, please share a copy of it with your friends. When you introduce something valuable to another person, they will associate that value with you. Not only will you become known as a giver, but you'll be helping the people around you to level up and create meaningful change in their lives. How cool is that?

PART IV:

Healthy, Wealthy, and Happy Habits

12. Healthy Habits

Drink More Water

Why: Studies show roughly 75% of Americans drink less than the recommended amount of water per day.[22] Although the research varies based on gender, age, height, weight, and activity level, most people should be drinking 10 to 15 cups of water daily. One way to understand how important it is to be drinking enough water is to think, "If I am not drinking enough water, I am intentionally looking for the opposite of all of these benefits."

Expected Health Benefits of Drinking More Water:

- Improves energy levels
- Improves brain function
- Improves physical performance
- Improves mood
- Regulates body temperature
- Protects tissue, spine, and joints
- Helps excrete waste
- Improves nutrient absorption
- Supports weight loss
- Helps digestive system
- Prevents headaches
- Prevents hangovers from alcohol
- Prevents constipation
- Prevents dehydration

My Experience: This behavior was very easy to adopt. Rather than filling up a dozen water bottles or cups per day, I purchased a one-gallon bottle online. This way, I only have to fill my bottle once or twice per day and it becomes very easy to track the amount I've had. In terms of benefits, I feel better both physically and mentally when I am hydrated.

Pro Tip: If you're having trouble enjoying water and find it a burden to drink, try adding a powdered health supplement, trace minerals, or fruit. Now, your water includes all the health benefits above plus the intended benefit of the substance you're adding.

> *"Drinking water is like washing out your insides. The water will cleanse the system, fill you up, decrease your caloric load and improve the function of all your tissues."*[23]
> —Kevin R. Stone, advanced orthopedic surgeon and author of *Play Forever*

Morning Sun Exposure

Why: As humans, we all have an internal process called a circadian rhythm that regulates our sleep-wake cycles. This rhythm repeats every 24 hours and is controlled by sun exposure. Many sleep inefficiencies stem from a disrupted circadian rhythm because we aren't getting outside in the mornings and exposing ourselves to the sun. When the sun goes down, our bodies naturally produce melatonin, which lowers anxiety and prepares us for sleep. For optimum sleep efficiency, you want those two pieces of the process to be differentiated and cycling naturally, just like it did before the invention of electricity. Sunlight has other benefits too, like kicking off the production of vitamin D, which helps maintain calcium levels and keeps our immune system operating well.

Expected Health Benefits of Morning Sun Exposure:

- Regulates circadian rhythm
- Produces vitamin D
- Maintains calcium levels
- Strengthens immune system
- Improves mood
- Improves energy
- Lowers blood pressure
- Heals skin inflammation
- Prevents some types of cancer
- Prevents mood disorders

My Experience: Although getting outside for some morning sun exposure can be tough during the winter months, I found it easy to adopt because of how great it makes me feel. Whenever I am unable to get outside in the morning even for just 15 minutes, I can feel it later in the day as my energy levels decrease and I get sleepy around mid-afternoon.

Pro Tip: By stacking this behavior with another beneficial morning habit like exercise, you can kill two birds with one stone. Don't wear sunglasses for the first couple of minutes, as your eyes are the primary receptors for sunlight. Thankfully, these benefits also hold true on cloudy days.

> *"Getting sunlight in your eyes first thing in the morning is vital to mental and physical health. It is perhaps the most important thing that all of us can and should do in order to promote metabolic well-being, promote the positive function of your hormone system, and get your mental health steering in the right direction."*[24]
>
> —Andrew Huberman, Ph.D., neuroscience professor and lab director at Stanford University

Artificial Light Exposure

Why: For all the same reasons listed above, it's important to expose yourself to light early in the morning. Like me, you might live in an area where it gets very cold and dark during certain times of the year. By keeping a light therapy lamp on your desk or next to your bed, you can compensate for the lack of real sunlight with artificial light, and gain many of the same benefits. I originally learned about these lights when a company named Circadian Optics demonstrated their artificial lights on ABC's *Shark Tank*.[25]

Expected Health Benefits of Artificial Sun Exposure:

- Regulates circadian rhythm
- Produces vitamin D
- Maintains calcium levels
- Strengthens immune system
- Improves mood

- Improves energy
- Lowers blood pressure
- Heals skin inflammation
- Prevents some types of cancer
- Prevents mood disorders

My Experience: When I received my Circadian Optics Light Therapy Lamp, I started using it immediately. It sits next to my computer monitor and I use it intermittently throughout my mornings. I have become a customer for life. Although it's tempting, try not to use this device in the afternoon as too much artificial sun exposure later in the day can delay the release of melatonin and make it harder to fall asleep at night. I try to mix this artificial light with real sun exposure so that I can get an extra dose of energy without having to spend additional time outside in the morning.

Pro Tip: If you're having trouble getting out of bed in the morning, it's likely that your room is still dark. I decided to get a second device from Circadian Optics and placed it right next to my bedside. Once my alarm goes off in the morning, I turn on the device and stare into the light for a minute or two. I am also a fan of a company called HumanCharger® that makes light-emitting earbuds that enable you to receive light through your ears to alleviate symptoms of 'winter blues.'

"Shorter daylight hours can affect sleep, productivity, and state of mind. Light therapy, also known as phototherapy, may help. It uses light boxes emitting full-spectrum light to simulate sunlight."[26]

—Andrew Weil, M.D.

Drink a Morning Cocktail

Why: Since we don't actively drink water while we sleep, most of us wake up dehydrated. Eight hours+ without water is a long time. In his book, *Own the Day, Own Your Life*, author Aubrey Marcus teaches his readers about a morning mineral cocktail he drinks every day to combat this problem. It's a mixture of water, lemon juice, and Himalayan salt. The water hydrates, the lemon adds some nutrients and taste, and the Himalayan salt adds a host of vitamins, minerals, and electrolytes.

Expected Health Benefits of Drinking a Morning Cocktail:

- Improves energy levels
- Improves brain function
- Improves physical performance
- Improves mood
- Regulates body temperature
- Protects tissue, spine, and joints
- Helps excrete waste
- Improves nutrient absorption
- Supports weight loss
- Helps digestive system
- Prevents headaches
- Prevents hangovers from alcohol
- Prevents constipation
- Prevents dehydration

My Experience: I was not a fan of the taste at first, but after experimenting with different ratios of ingredients, I found a mixture I looked forward to drinking each day. If you're someone who normally drinks coffee first thing in the morning, make it a rule to always have one of these cocktails before coffee. Aubrey compares kicking off your day with coffee to waking up with a fire alarm instead of a phone alarm. Be kind to your body and ease into your day the right way.

Pro Tip: Prepare your morning cocktail before you go to sleep so that it's ready to drink the moment you wake up. That way, you have no excuse if you're running late or feeling unmotivated. Also, don't add too much salt, as it can act as a diuretic, and you'll find yourself running to the bathroom. I learned that through trial and error!

> *"The first thing I do after waking up is hydrate. I get twelve ounces of room temperature spring water, a dash of Himalayan salt, and some lemon and crush it to rehydrate from the water I lost overnight."*[27]
> —Aubrey Marcus, author of *Own the Day, Own Your Life*

Optimize Your Coffee

Why: If you're like me and you drink coffee daily, you'll love this healthy habit. Let's say you drink two cups a day. That means you're going to drink roughly 22,000 cups over the next 30 years. Wow. The type of coffee you're drinking matters. I drink coffee made from Arabica beans (as opposed to Robusta) that has been tested for toxins, which can be found in a lot of low-quality coffees. I usually prepare my first cup of the day with grass-fed ghee butter (casein protein and lactose free) and C8 MCT oil (medium-chain triglycerides, highly efficient fuel sources for the body that improve mental clarity) as a replacement for breakfast so that I can stay in a fasted state of autophagy until lunchtime. (See Intermittent Fasting for more on autophagy.) These ingredients satisfy hunger, kick-start fat-burning, support cognitive function, and more.

Expected Health Benefits of Optimizing Your Coffee:

- Avoids harmful toxins
- Satisfies morning hunger
- Improves metabolism
- Improves brain function
- Avoids caffeine crashes
- Antioxidants protect cells

My Experience: I never really drank coffee until I visited Medellín, Colombia. After spending an afternoon at a small farm outside the city picking coffee and learning all about the characteristics of quality coffee, I became a coffee lover. And since I know I will likely consume 22,000 cups over the next 30 years, I try to optimize my coffee. Implementing this has been easy and I enjoy the taste of better coffee anyway. It can get a little expensive if you're increasing the cost per cup, but it's worth it in the long run. Plus, I haven't experienced an afternoon caffeine crash since I switched.

Pro Tip: I am happy that some of the most dedicated biohackers and health nuts like Dave Asprey (Bulletproof Coffee) and Ben Greenfield (Kion Coffee) sell ethically sourced, toxin-tested, high-quality Arabica beans. When you buy from them, you know you're buying the best health-conscious coffee you can. Plus, Arabica beans typically have less caffeine than Robusta beans, which means you can drink more of it and take advantage of the natural antioxidants that all coffee varieties possess.

> *"Biohacking is all about taking full control of your biology, which includes discovering ways to improve the ordinary things you do in your everyday life, like drinking coffee."*[28]
> —Dave Asprey, four-time *New York Times* best-selling science author

No Caffeine After Midday

Why: Caffeine is a double-edged sword. It keeps you alert and awake by blocking sleep-promoting receptors in your brain called adenosine receptors, which is great for the morning but terrible for the evening. Around 50% of the caffeine the average person consumes is still circulating in the body six hours after consumption. In total, it can take up to 10 hours to completely clear it from your bloodstream. Since I care so much about my sleep habits, I avoid caffeine after midday because I want it to be out of my system a couple of hours before I go to sleep.

Expected Health Benefits of Avoiding Caffeine After Midday:

- Improves sleep latency
- Improves overall sleep time
- Improves sleep efficiency
- Improves percentage of deep sleep
- Reduces sleep apnea
- Reduces impact on sleep cycles

My Experience: When I first started my reading journey, I stayed up late and got a lot of reading done on weeknights. During that time, I supplemented with caffeine to stay awake. After reading about caffeine's impact on sleep, however, I immediately stopped consuming it after midday. The transition was rough at first, but now, you couldn't pay me to drink it in the late afternoon or evening. The fact that I used to drink alcohol mixed with soda (caffeine) all night and still fall asleep blows my mind.

Pro Tip: If you're working long hours and looking for an alternative to caffeine, try supplementing with nicotine or L-theanine. According to Dave Asprey, nicotine enhances coordination, vigilance, memory, and reaction time.[29] There are much safer ways to consume nicotine than cigarettes, including nicotine gum, mints, and toothpicks. Caffeine is the most widely used drug in the world, yet nicotine is the one down upon. Be careful, since both are highly addictive.

> *"Caffeine has an average half-life of five to seven hours. Let's say that you have a cup of coffee after your evening dinner, around 7:30 p.m. This means that by 1:30 a.m., 50% of that caffeine may still be active and circulating throughout your brain tissue. In other words, by 1:30 a.m., you're only halfway to completing the job of cleansing your brain of the caffeine you drank after dinner."*[30]
> —Matthew Walker, professor of neuroscience at UC Berkeley, and author of *Why We Sleep*

Intermittent Fasting

Why: This is the first time in human history that we have unlimited access to food, especially unhealthy ones that cause inflammation. In the past, the average person could go weeks without eating, which had a lot of benefits. Today, prolonged fasting, sometimes for as little as 12 or 16 hours depending on your metabolism, causes the body to enter a state of repair called autophagy.[31] During this time, instead of focusing on digestion and healing the inflammation caused by food, your body can clean out damaged cells to regenerate newer, healthier cells. Taking a break from consuming calories has several other benefits associated with it as well.

Expected Health Benefits of Intermittent Fasting:

- Burns more fat
- Increases natural human growth hormone (HGH)
- Repairs cells
- Reduces blood sugar
- Reduces inflammation
- Reduces oxidative stress
- Improves heart health
- Reduces risk of cancer
- Reduces risk of Alzheimer's
- Improves cognitive function
- Extends life span

My Experience: As someone who loves breakfast, this was hard for me to adopt. For the first couple of weeks, I was very hungry in the morning and would spend a lot of time thinking about food. After a while, though, the hunger stopped, and I noticed a significant drop in inflammation throughout my body. Aches and pains went away. Now, I rarely consume food before 12:00 p.m. (noon) or after 7:00 p.m.

Pro Tip: If you're struggling with hunger in the mornings, try the coffee recipe I described in the Optimize Your Coffee section. The ghee butter and C8 MCT oil suppress hunger and because neither contains carbs or protein, you'll stay in that fasted state of autophagy and cognitive clarity. Make sure you drink a lot of water too.

> *"Intermittent fasting is incredibly useful in aiding fat loss, preventing cancer, building muscle, and increasing resilience. Done correctly, it's one of the most painless high-impact ways to live longer."*[32]
> —Dave Asprey, four-time *New York Times* best-selling science author

Exercise in the Morning

Why: When you exercise, your body releases chemicals called endorphins that interact with the receptors in your brain to trigger positive feelings, improve your mood and self-esteem, and decrease stress. Since these endorphins can last up to 16 hours, depending on the duration and intensity of the exercise, wouldn't you want to reap the benefits all day instead of wasting them asleep? Plus, exercise has a myriad other common benefits, like weight loss, energy boost, better sleep, and more.

Expected Health Benefits of Exercising in the Morning:

- Increases endorphins
- Boosts weight loss
- Improves mood
- Improves self-esteem
- Improves heart health
- Improves cognitive function
- Improves immune system
- Increases metabolic rate
- Decreases feelings of stress
- Tones and firms muscles

My Experience: I have been exercising for as long as I can remember, but for most of my life, I exercised in the evenings. After reading about the benefits of exercising in the morning, however, I shifted to morning workouts and never looked back. I feel better throughout the day and really enjoy the peace and quiet I can only get during exercising first thing.

Pro Tip: If you're struggling to find time to work out in the morning, try doing it at home. There are countless bodyweight exercises and outdoor cardio sessions, or HIIT (high-intensity interval training) classes on YouTube that can be done in 15 to 30 minutes so that they don't disrupt your day. Even if you also want to work out in the afternoon or evening, you should still try to get a quick morning session in. When you combine the advantages of morning sun exposure with morning exercise, you'll be compounding the benefits.

> *"I start off with exercise first thing in the morning. It increases my energy and releases endorphins, so I feel great."*[33]
> —Robin Sharma, author of *The 5 AM Club*

Take Supplements

Why: Despite our best efforts, it's almost impossible to get an optimum amount of nutrients from food alone. Supplements bridge this gap and ensure we are covering the bases every day. Common supplements include vitamins, minerals, and herbal products. We consume them to maintain or improve our health. As we age, our ability to break down and absorb nutrients declines, which is another reason to supplement, since we'll require more than we can eat. As today's farming techniques continue to deplete soil, the food we consume from most grocery stores lacks nutrient density. Eating organic produce helps, but just like most people fail to drink enough water, most also fail to consume enough of some of the most essential vitamins and minerals. Studies[34] have shown that roughly 50% of Americans are deficient in vitamins A, C, and D, and magnesium. The benefits to consuming these common vitamins are endless. Do some research yourself and talk to a nutritionist about what supplements can benefit you.

Expected Health Benefits of Taking Supplements:
- Improves mood and energy
- Boosts immune system and biological processes
- Slows aging

My Experience: I used to think taking additional vitamins was a waste of my money until I read widely on the subject. Although it can get expensive, the benefits to supplementing are seemingly endless. As the saying goes, healthy people have a thousand wishes, whereas sick people only have one.

Pro Tip: If you're finding it difficult to keep up with lots of supplements, consider something like Athletic Greens®. Their product supports gut health, immunity, energy, recovery, focus, aging, and more, all in one daily drink mix. I now use this product to replace many of the individual supplements I was originally taking.

> *"Getting all of the nutrients you need simply cannot be done without supplements."*[35]
>
> —Steven Gundry, M.D., author of *The Plant Paradox*

Take Cold Showers

Why: Just like morning exercise, cold showers release endorphins that interact with the receptors in your brain to trigger positive feelings, improve your mood and self-esteem, and decrease stress. This jolt to your system sends electrical impulses to your brain that can also increase alertness, clarity, and energy levels. Cold showers assist in weight loss by increasing your metabolism, and cause your body to work a bit harder to maintain its core temperature, which improves circulation. Finally, cold showers stimulate leukocytes, better known as white blood cells, which help your body counteract common illnesses, like the cold and the flu.

Expected Health Benefits of Taking Cold Showers:

- Increases endorphins
- Boosts weight loss
- Improves mood
- Improves self-esteem
- Improves heart health

- Improves cognitive function
- Improves immune system
- Improves circulation
- Decreases feelings of stress
- Increases willpower

My Experience: Burr! In the beginning, I would finish my showers with a burst of cold water and then gradually, I worked my way up to full cold showers. At first, the willpower required to turn the handle to cold was enormous, but I did it anyway and was eventually able to desensitize myself to it. This increase in willpower is transferable to other areas of your life—you'll become fearless. The electric feeling after a cold shower is incredible. Now, I can't get enough of them! I recently decided to take this practice to the next level with ice baths. These are more difficult, but I feel amazing after I'm done.

Pro Tip: If you're like me, and you really struggle with this one, try a specialized breathing technique called the Wim Hof Method right before you crank the water to cold. You'll barely feel the water. I'll explain this technique more in the Breathwork Healthy Habit section, but you can Google it now if you're interested.

> *"After a cold shower in the morning, you feel much more centered during the rest of your day. Try it out and see what it does for you."*[36]
> —Wim Hof, Dutch extreme athlete, holder of over 20 world records, and author of *The Wim Hof Method*

Use a Standing Desk

Why: Have you heard the saying, "Sitting is the new smoking?" Well, although I think that is a bit of an exaggeration, sitting too much is seriously bad for health. People who sit a lot every day have an increased risk of conditions, like diabetes and heart disease.[37] Humans are mobile creatures and sitting stagnant for eight hours a day is terrible for us. By switching to a standing desk, you lower your risk for weight gain and obesity because you're burning more calories. How many more calories? Sixty-four calories per eight-hour workday, which, over the course of 250 workdays per year, is 16,000 calories, or the equivalent to over 4lbs of fat. Not bad, huh?

Expected Health Benefits of Using a Standing Desk:

- Improves mood
- Improves energy
- Decreases risk of heart disease
- Decreases risk of diabetes
- Decreases risk of weight gain
- Reduces back pain

My Experience: I decided to switch to a standing desk after interviewing author Vanessa Van Edwards. She had such energy during our talk, so I asked what her secret was. She revealed that it was her standing desk, so I made the switch for myself and am thrilled with the decision. My energy during video calls and while recording podcasts or other forms of content has improved dramatically.

Pro Tip: Not sure if you want to commit? Purchase an adjustable desk that can shift from sitting height to standing height. This way, you can ease into your decision by standing for the morning and sitting for the afternoon as you get used to it. I use an ApexDesk and really love it. I also added a movable desk treadmill so that I can walk leisurely while I'm working. You'll barely even notice that you're walking, but you'll be improving blood flow and burning some extra calories while you do it.

> *"Sitting is more dangerous than smoking, kills more people than HIV, and is more treacherous than parachuting. We are sitting ourselves to death."*[38]
>
> —James Levine, M.D., Ph.D., professor of medicine at the Mayo Clinic

Optimize Your Gum

Why: At first glance, this might seem out of place, but chewing gum has many benefits. For one, chewing gum reduces the buildup of plaque. Plaque carries bacteria that will damage tooth enamel and lead to cavities. You can also burn up to 11 calories per hour while chewing gum, which, as we know, adds up over time. Chewing gum improves blood flow, fights sleepiness, and increases saliva production, which will help prevent nausea and heartburn.[39] If all of that wasn't enough, some gum manufacturers now add vitamins and stimulants to their gum so that you can compound the benefits. These are substances, like caffeine for energy, L-theanine for focus, and B-vitamins for cell health and energy levels.

Expected Health Benefits of Optimizing Your Gum:

- Reduces buildup of plaque
- Burns calories
- Improves blood flow
- Reduces drowsiness
- Increases saliva production
- Prevents nausea and heartburn
- Added vitamins and stimulants boost energy levels and cell health

My Experience: As someone who chews gum daily, optimizing my gum was a no-brainer. I chew Neuro Gum in the morning, which contains added stimulants to boost mental endurance. This is especially useful in situations where I can't have my normal morning coffee, like on planes, or long car rides.

Pro Tip: Although chewing gum with sugar doesn't pose major health risks, it should be avoided. Just like calories burned add up over time, so does sugar. Look for sugar-free gum that contains natural sweeteners and flavorings, like citric acid, to maximize the reduction of plaque.

> *"I've been chewing this Neuro Gum. It's gum with nootropics in it...*
> *It's got a little bit of caffeine, L-theanine and B-vitamins... I love it."*[40]
> —Joe Rogan, host of *The Joe Rogan Experience* podcast

Test Food Sensitivities

Why: Food allergies happen when the immune system, our body's defense system, perceives a certain food as a threat. Each of us has a unique microbiome, the collective of bacteria, archaea, viruses, and fungi that make up our gut, which means that each of us has varying sensitivity to different types of food. When you consume something that doesn't agree with your gut, your body reacts by triggering inflammation. The unpleasant symptoms related to food sensitivities can include fatigue, migraines, bloating, depression, and skin problems. Most people unknowingly eat foods that trigger inflammation every day, which causes the body to fight unnecessary fights daily. Prolonged inflammation is associated with heart disease, diabetes, certain cancers, arthritis, and bowel disease.[41] By testing your food sensitivities and cutting out foods that cause inflammation, you can reduce and even eliminate the symptoms mentioned above and allow your body to rest.

Expected Health Benefits of Testing Food Sensitivities (and eliminating bad foods):

- Decreases allergy symptoms
- Decreases inflammation
- Decreases risk of heart disease
- Decreases risk of diabetes
- Decreases risk of cancers
- Increases cellular repair

My Experience: When I purchased a food sensitivity test from Everlywell I was shocked to see how many foods I was eating on a regular basis that were causing inflammation. I had literally been poisoning myself, sometimes three times per day for months on end with foods like eggs and Brussels sprouts. I immediately eliminated the worst foods and quickly started seeing the differences in my energy levels. Now I know what not to eat and almost never feel bloated after a meal.

Pro Tip: Your gut bacteria is always changing, meaning your food sensitivities are going to change over time as well. Testing every couple of years and dynamically adjusting your diet is always worth it.

> *"Eating healthy food fills your body with energy and nutrients.*
> *Imagine your cells smiling back at you and saying: 'Thank you!'"*[42]
> —Karen Salmansohn, author of *Happy Habits*

Playful Cardio

Why: Do you enjoy running? If you do, lucky you. If you're like me and you can't stand this standard cardio workout, I would encourage you to implement something I call "playful cardio." Playful cardio gives you all the health benefits of normal cardio, but without the boredom. It comes in many forms. For me, it includes playing football and basketball with my friends, swimming at the beach, going on long walks or bike rides with my wife, and fun excursions while traveling, like snorkeling and hiking. Other activities you could do include jumping rope, dancing, boxing, rock climbing, and obstacle courses. Playful cardio can be done alone or with other people. The options are limitless, and they are always enjoyable.

Expected Health Benefits of Playful Cardio:

- Improves joint health
- Improves muscle function
- Helps weight management
- Improves pancreas, lung, and heart health
- Improves sexual function
- Boosts mood
- Improves your sleep
- Boosts energy

My Experience: This was game-changing for me as someone who dislikes running on a treadmill. Now, I am constantly searching for new ways to get my cardio in and most of the things I come up with are group activities I can do with my wife. Win-win!

Pro Tip: Schedule playful cardio sessions into your week just like you would with a standard gym workout. By scheduling them, you'll have no excuse but to participate and get your heart rate up! Sessions can work as social outings, meetups with friends, or dates. When I travel to new places, I am always looking for fun activities to engage in.

> *"Cardio is a nice way to start the morning, man. Whether you sit on the bike for half an hour or throw on two jumpers and just sweat, it's good to get up, get the body active, put on your headphones, and just pedal away."*[43]
>
> —Anthony Joshua, professional boxer

Purify Your Indoor Air

Why: Most of us work, relax, and sleep indoors. Our homes provide protection from outside threats and harsh weather, but they can also expose us to many different forms of airborne pollutants. VOCs (volatile organic compounds), like cleaning products; biological pollutants, like bacteria, dust, pollen, animal dander, etc.; combustion byproducts, like carbon monoxide; and legacy pollutants, like lead and mercury, can impact your health in very negative ways. I first learned about airborne pollutants while I was researching sleep. Many people sleep in environments that cause sleep apnea and other sleep disorders without even realizing it. By purifying the air in your home and workspace, you can dramatically reduce the impact of these pollutants on your health.

Expected Health Benefits of Purifying Your Indoor Air:
- Decreases asthma symptoms
- Eliminates airborne pollutants
- Neutralizes unpleasant odors
- Reduces risk of airborne disease
- Improves sleep

My Experience: A few years ago, I purchased a few snake plants for my bedroom. As well as producing oxygen, these plants absorb toxins from the air through their leaves. Fewer toxins and more oxygen? Count me in. One of the reasons I chose snake plants is that they are hard to kill, easy to maintain, and I find them visually appealing. Now, I have a bunch of them in my office too.

Pro Tip: I decided to take it to the next level by purchasing a couple of air purifier machines with HEPA (high-efficiency particulate absorbing) technology. They remove 99.7% of the airborne pollutants that pass through them. They aren't too expensive and, although they don't look as nice as the plants, I am sure they work more efficiently to clean the air around me.

> *"Plants are solar-powered air purifiers whose filter never needs replacing."*
>
> —Unknown

Breathe Through Your Nose

Why: Breathing is one of those things to which we give very little conscious thought. We all breathe, all the time, automatically. Well, you might be surprised to hear that there are many benefits to breathing through your nose instead of your mouth, both while you're awake and especially while you're asleep. Our noses are designed to help us breathe safely and efficiently because of their ability to filter out foreign particles, humidify inhaled air, and produce nitric oxide. Mouth breathing, on the other hand, increases your risk of inhaling unfiltered air, allergic reactions to airborne allergens, dry mouth, tooth decay, and sleep apnea/snoring. According to James Nestor, author of *Breath*, mouth breathing can lead the bones of the face to develop differently, causing flatter features, drooping eyes, a narrow dental arch, and a small chin.[44] Lastly, nasal breathing keeps air in your lungs longer than mouth breathing, which means that up to 20% more oxygen can enter your bloodstream.

Expected Health Benefits of Breathing Through Your Nose:

- Reduces exposure to allergens
- Increases nitric oxide
- Decreases bad breath and dry mouth
- Decreases risk of tooth decay
- Decreases risk of sleep apnea
- Improves your immune system
- Corrects facial structure
- Absorbs more oxygen

My Experience: After reading *Breath*, I was shocked to learn how important nasal breathing is. There is almost no reason to breathe through your mouth unless you're speaking or eating or have a cold. Seriously. For the last couple of years now, I have made a conscious effort to breathe through my nose and, funny enough, my allergies have decreased dramatically.

Pro Tip: I have always been a mouth breather, and that translated to my sleep as well. I knew sleep apnea was caused by disrupted airways and mouth breathing, so I tried everything to stop it. Chin straps, mouth guards, and even some wearable devices. What worked the best? For a while, I used a small piece of surgical tape to keep my mouth closed at night. Now, I use a strong form of mouth tape from a company called Hostage Tape. I love their product and use it every night.

> *"Breathe through your nose all the time."*[45]
>
> —James Nestor, author of *Breath*

Hold Your Breath

Why: Somewhere along the border of Poland and the Czech Republic lives a man named Wim Hof. Known as "The Iceman," Wim has developed a breathing technique called the Wim Hof Method, or WHM. Supported by decades of self-exploration and groundbreaking scientific studies, this exercise has a host of health benefits. It simply involves rhythmic inhales and exhales followed by holding your breath for minutes at a time. Look up the method online and follow the guided instructions—you'll amaze yourself. Wim often combines this breathing exercise with cold exposure, which increasing the health benefits. He holds several world records including climbing Mount Kilimanjaro in shorts, running a half marathon above the Arctic Circle barefoot, and standing in a container while covered with ice cubes for over 112 minutes. Impressive.[46]

Expected Health Benefits of the WHM:

- Improves energy
- Decreases stress
- Supports immune system
- Improves willpower
- Improves focus
- Improves sleep

My Experience: I first discovered Wim while reading *Tools of Titans* by Tim Ferriss. I was blown away. Using the WHM, Tim has his readers go through an exercise where you can dramatically improve your max number of push-ups. Mine doubled. Now, I use the WHM on a regular basis and methodically hit three-minute breath holds.

Pro Tip: Wim has a mobile app you can use for the breathing portion of his framework. It tracks your data and gives you structure. I highly recommend trying it. You will be surprised how powerful your breath truly is and how it controls so many areas of your life.

"Power is within us all. Anything can be overcome by going within."[47]
—Wim Hof, author of *The Wim Hof Method*

Stretch Your Body

Why: The first thing that comes to mind for most people when they think of stretching is a runner limbering up before a run or a gymnast about to perform. What most people don't realize is that stretching has a host of day-to-day benefits, keeping our muscles and joints healthy. If you want to be active later in life without feeling pain or tension every time you walk up a set of stairs, it's important to get into the habit of stretching your muscles, and keeping them long, lean, and flexible. Stretching techniques come in all shapes and sizes, so do a little research and find a routine that fits your needs and ability.

Expected Health Benefits of Stretching Your Body:

- Increases flexibility
- Increases range of motion
- Increases blood flow
- Improves posture
- Improves physical performance
- Prevents back pain
- Prevents muscle and joint injuries
- Reduces stress
- Improves sleep

My Experience: Growing up, I always thought stretching before a workout or sporting event was a waste of time. Nowadays, after some injuries that could have easily been prevented by improving my flexibility, I don't take it for granted. I experiment with different types of stretching all the time including practicing yoga. My body always feels better when I am flexible and if I lose momentum and stop stretching, I can always feel it after a couple of weeks. If you implement a standing desk, you'll be more likely to stretch during your workday too.

Pro Tip: If you're looking to radically improve your range of motion, try gravity yoga, wherein you hold your stretches for one to ten minutes at a time. These stretching workouts are intense and will leave you feeling sore, but they are well worth it. I try to combine my daily stretching with morning sun exposure, right before my morning exercise.

> *"I have missed two days of stretching now in five years."*[48]
> —David Goggins, author of *Can't Hurt Me*

Optimize Your Smile

Why: When I say, "optimizing your smile," I am really talking about implementing a few different oral health habits. First, although it might sound basic, you should be flossing daily, or at least a few times a week. Flossing gets rid of plaque, reduces your risk of cavities, prevents gum disease, reduces bad breath, and more. Second, I recommend oil pulling. Oil pulling is the ancient way of cleaning your mouth and simply involves taking an oil, like coconut oil, and swishing it around your mouth and through your teeth for five to 10 minutes. It has all the same benefits as flossing, but it can also kill additional bacteria in your mouth—and it tastes better. Third, correct jaw misalignment. There are countless benefits, including a balanced appearance to your face, better function of your teeth, improvement in speech, reduction of headaches, and better sleep. Lastly, scrape your tongue. It might sound strange, but over time, a lot of debris, bacteria, and dead cells can build up on it. By using a tongue scraper, you can improve your sense of taste and the appearance of your tongue and remove bacteria.

Expected Health Benefits of Optimizing Your Smile:

- Reduces plaque
- Reduces risk of cavities
- Prevents gum disease
- Reduces bad breath
- Reduces mouth bacteria
- Balances facial structure
- Improves teeth function
- Improves sleep

My Experience: Despite my parents' best efforts at regulating my mouth hygiene, it was average at best while I was growing up. Now, after learning about the importance of flossing, oil pulling, and tongue scraping, I have made them a regular part of my routine. I can't go more than a day without flossing and I am often complimented on my smile.

Pro Tip: We all brush our teeth, but not all toothbrushes are created equal. Electronic toothbrushes clean your teeth, gums, and tongue more thoroughly than manual brushes and require a lot less effort.

"Nothing you wear is more important than your smile."[49]
—Connie Stevens, actress

Sweat More

Why: Our skin is our largest organ—biohackers refer to it as our "third kidney." The sweat glands in our skin filter out toxins, which boosts our immune system. Sweat also cools our body and helps us maintain optimum body temperature. When we work out intensely or sit in a sauna, our body sweats more to cool down. Sweating increases circulation, can prevent kidney stones due to toxin build-up, increases thirst, leading us to drink more water, and opens pores, which reduces skin problems such as acne.

Expected Health Benefits of Sweating:
- Detoxifies the body
- Increases circulation
- Prevents kidney stones
- Improves immune system

My Experience: After reading about the benefits of sweating, I started spending time in my gym's dry sauna after each workout. I quickly fell in love with the experience—especially after a night out drinking alcohol. In a 10- to 20-minute session at around 200°F, I would be covered head to toe in sweat. As this became a regular activity, I noticed I got colds less often and when I did, I recovered much faster. I have now experimented with other types of saunas, including the wet and infrared varieties.

Pro Tip: If getting to a gym is inconvenient, I recommend purchasing an infrared at-home sauna. The one I use encapsulates my body but allows my head and arms to stick out. This way, my body sweats, yet I can still read a book or use my phone during the process. Eventually, I will purchase a dry sauna for my home, but it can get expensive.

> *"The sauna robustly elevates heat shock protein levels that can persist for up to 48 hours. Heat shock proteins play a preventive role in neurodegenerative diseases and sauna use is associated with a 66% lower risk of Alzheimer's."*[50]
>
> —Dr. Rhonda Patrick, Ph.D.

Take Epsom Salt Baths

Why: Epsom salt is a naturally occurring mineral made up of magnesium and sulfate. When mixed with warm bath water, the magnesium and sulfates are absorbed by your skin and offer a host of health benefits. Low magnesium levels are linked to nerve damage and can increase your risk of high blood pressure and heart disease, so Epsom salt baths are a good way to restore levels within your body. Magnesium also increases serotonin, which is a factor in lowering stress levels.

Expected Health Benefits of Taking Epsom Salt Baths:

- Reduces stress
- Prevents nerve dysfunction
- Lowers blood pressure
- Reduces risk of heart disease
- Reduces inflammation
- Reduces muscle soreness
- Relieves constipation
- Improves circulation

My Experience: Growing up, I was not fond of taking baths, so I felt some resistance to this when I first read about it. Over time, though, I began to love the calming environment and found the bath to be a great place to get some reading done. Note: it's much easier to read a Kindle than a paperback while soaking. The humidity can mess up your book's binding, so pages come loose. Just don't drop the device.

Pro Tip: Nowadays, you can buy Epsom salts blended with other substances such as lavender, eucalyptus, melatonin, and vitamins or minerals. Not only do they smell good, but they can also offer additional health benefits. I find myself soaking in these baths at least once per week, especially when I've been working out a lot and am looking to recover faster.

> *"There must be quite a few things that a hot bath won't cure, but I don't know many of them."*[51]
>
> —Sylvia Plath, poet and novelist

Try an Acupressure Mat

Why: Acupressure is an ancient Chinese therapy that offers many health benefits. Picture lying face up on a spiky mat full of small plastic points. For the first couple of minutes, you'll feel a slight pain and the urge to get off the mat. Then, you start to sense additional blood flow to areas of contact and a slight tingly sensation. After that, you'll feel warmth as your body softens and then…you're in a state of bliss. These mats are non-invasive, unlike acupuncture, and act as a form of natural pain relief.

Expected Health Benefits of Using an Acupressure Mat:

- Improves circulation
- Lowers blood pressure
- Relaxes your muscles
- Offers pain relief
- Releases endorphins
- Reduces stress

My Experience: Ouch! My first experience with one of these mats was shocking. During the first minute or two, I wondered why the packaging recommended 15 to 20 minutes. Just as described above, though, I soon felt a tingling sensation and was then transported to a state of pure bliss. The mat works wonders. I try to use it weekly, especially on my back. The targeted increase in blood flow is wonderful for releasing tension and speeding up recovery after working out.

Pro Tip: Experiment with different parts of your body. These mats are often advertised for your back, but they can also be used on your neck, stomach, and feet. I had always been a bit skeptical about acupuncture and acupressure, but was shocked to see how fast I saw results. These mats are a cheap and effective way to feel better.

> *"Acupressure can be effective in helping relieve headaches, eyestrain, sinus problems, neck pain, backaches, arthritis, muscle aches, and tension due to stress."*[52]
>
> —Michael Reed Gach, Ph.D., author of *Acupressure's Potent Points*

Always Take the Stairs

Why: A few years ago, I listened to an internet entrepreneur talk about a decision he made to "always take the stairs" instead of the escalator or elevator, which has no positive impact on your health. His reasoning? Well, climbing stairs is good for you. Escalators and elevators are amazing inventions, especially for those unable to walk upstairs or for people working on the top floors of massive office buildings—walking up 10+ flights of stairs is time-consuming, and you don't want to show up sweating to a meeting. Outside those extenuating circumstances, however, I recommend that you too "always take the stairs."

Expected Health Benefits of Always Taking the Stairs:

- Improves blood flow
- Improves muscle strength
- Burns calories
- Increases bone density
- Improves flexibility
- Boosts energy

My Experience: This rule comes into play more than you would think—I always take the stairs in public places, such as airports, malls, and restaurants. Not only does it feel good, but I can often move much faster than everyone using the escalators next to me. Now, I take pride in finding the stairs and using them while a lot of people avoid them.

Pro Tip: Put some rules in place. Personally, I will always default to using the stairs if I am climbing less than 10 floors. That way, I don't have to make a choice each time I approach an escalator or elevator that brings me somewhere less than 10 floors away. Carrying a suitcase up a flight of stairs is never fun, but it's a good workout. I always think about the calorie difference between taking the stairs and taking the elevator, and then multiply it by the thousands of times I will make this decision throughout my life. That's where the major benefit comes from.

> *"Success comes down to choosing the hard right over the easy wrong. Consistently."*[53]
>
> —Rory Vaden, author of *Take the Stairs*

Track Your Sleep

Why: Improving your sleep is hard to measure because you're not able to consciously observe yourself and how you're feeling while you're asleep. So how do you know if the activities you implement are making a difference? Well, as management thinker Peter Drucker is often quoted as saying, "You can't manage what you can't measure." Thankfully, there have been massive improvements in sleep tracking technology over the past few years. These devices will tell you if the other changes you're making are improving the different aspects of your sleep, such as REM sleep, deep sleep, awake time, and more.

Expected Health Benefit of Tracking Your Sleep:
* Certainty around whether the healthy habits you're implementing are improving your sleep

My Experience: I started tracking my sleep with a Fitbit a few years ago. It was interesting to see the data, but I didn't really know what it meant. After reading *Why We Sleep* by Dr. Matthew Walker, sleep became much more important to me, and I made the effort to understand the metrics. I have been using an Oura Ring for the last three years now, and I'm a big fan of the data it gives me. One of the first things I do every morning is check my sleep statistics.

Pro Tip: Whenever I implement a new sleep-related habit, such as a change to my nighttime routine, sleep supplements, or overall diet, I monitor my sleep stats to see if there is a measured improvement. Otherwise, how do you know if you're making progress? Drucker's quote reminds us that unless we are defining goals and measuring against them, we can't know if we are successful or not. Moral of the story? Start tracking your sleep!

> *"By monitoring your sleep patterns, you can see how much quality sleep you're getting. This kind of valuable information empowers you to take control of your sleep and optimize your sleep experience."*[54]
> —Dr. Kimberly VanBuren, marriage and family therapist

Sleep in Total Darkness

Why: Light is one of the most important factors affecting sleep. Photoreceptors in your eyes, which absorb light, play the largest role in regulating your circadian rhythm (aka your sleep/wake cycle). By exposing yourself to light, you can disrupt your sleep cycle and confuse your circadian rhythm. It's well documented that even moonlight will negatively impact your sleep efficiency, decrease your deep sleep, and delay your REM sleep. By installing blackout curtains, which block up to 99% of light, you can improve your sleep quality at night and well into the morning, if you choose. The same goes for turning off devices that emit light inside your bedroom, such as televisions and phones. You can even buy blackout stickers to cover up the small lights that stay on all the time, such as on TVs and computer monitors, even when they are turned off.

Expected Health Benefit of Installing Blackout Curtains:
* Reduces disruptions during your sleep

My Experience: Installing blackout curtains and blackout stickers was a no-brainer for me, and I am happy I did it. Our ancestors slept in dark caves with no access to electricity, and I want to recreate that environment every night when I choose to sleep.

Pro Tip: If you're like me and you're constantly traveling, always bring a blackout eye mask with you so that you can recreate total darkness wherever you go. It is a cheap and effective way to improve your sleep. I usually double up and wear my eye mask while I'm sleeping in my blacked out room so that I keep up the habit.

> *"The shorter your sleep, the shorter your life. The leading causes of disease and death in developed nations—diseases that are crippling health-care systems, such as heart disease, obesity, dementia, diabetes, and cancer—all have recognized causal links to a lack of sleep."*[55]
> —Matthew Walker, professor of neuroscience at UC Berkeley, and author of *Why We Sleep*

Sleep With a White Noise Machine

Why: A white noise machine is a device that produces steady and continuous calming noises, such as the sound of rain or the wind blowing through trees. Use these machines at night to mask noises inside or outside your sleeping environment that might otherwise disrupt your sleep. Instead of waking up each time your partner goes to the bathroom, or the birds start chirping outside your window, you can maintain a peaceful, distraction-free environment in your bedroom.

Expected Health Benefit of Using a White Noise Machine:
- Reduces disruptions during your sleep

My Experience: I have been using the same white noise machine for several years now and I love it. Sort of like Pavlov's dog, I have trained myself to fall asleep shortly after I turn my machine on. A few times, I forgot to bring my device with me while traveling and I noticed the considerable difference. Thankfully, several great mobile apps also produce white noise. Be sure to charge your phone before letting it play for eight hours straight.

Pro Tip: If you want to take things to the next level, try playing binaural beats through headphones while you sleep. These use slightly different frequencies of tone, one in each ear, to create different auditory illusions. Some claim these sounds put your body into a deeper state of sleep and relaxation.[56] I tried this tip a few times but did not pursue it enough to see if there was an impact, since I did not enjoy sleeping with headphones.

> *"High-quality sleep fortifies your immune system, balances your hormones, boosts your metabolism, increases physical energy, and improves the function of your brain."*[57]
> —Shawn Stevenson, author of *Sleep Smarter*

Use a Weighted Blanket

Why: Weighted blankets are heavy blankets, usually between 5 and 50lbs, used for therapeutic purposes. The added weight is designed to produce a calming effect on the body, sort of like being hugged by another person, releasing oxytocin and other "feel-good" chemicals, and slowing your heart rate. This deep pressure stimulation relaxes the nervous system, eases anxiety, and can produce a feeling of well-being. Although you could also use these blankets during the day, using them at night, when they reduce your nighttime movement. They have been shown to lead to more restful sleep.

Expected Health Benefits of Using a Weighted Blanket:
- Releases oxytocin
- Reduces heart rate
- Reduces anxiety

My Experience: Weighted blankets are fun. I can remember receiving my first one in the mail. The box was huge and, as expected, heavy—it weighed 25lbs. The sensation of crawling under a weighted blanket before going to sleep is very comforting, and I would highly recommend it. Although they can be a pain to wash, I will probably be using one for the rest of my life.

Pro Tip: Try out different weights and find something that produces the desired effect for you. Currently, I use a 25lb weighted blanket on my bed, but I want to try something a bit heavier soon. I will then use my Oura Ring to see if a heavier blanket makes a difference to my sleep quality.

> *"Weighted blankets use deep-pressure stimulation, which is thought to stimulate the production of a mood-boosting hormone (serotonin), reduce the stress hormone (cortisol), and increase levels of melatonin, the hormone that helps you sleep."*[58]
> —Daniel Noyed, certified sleep science coach with SleepFoundation.org

Sleep in Colder Temperatures

Why: Going back to the caveman analogy, humans evolved sleeping outside. Outdoors, temperatures are typically lowest in the middle of the night and highest in the middle of the day. The science is clear: most humans reach deeper stages of sleep more effectively when sleeping at a cooler ambient temperature. Different studies suggest different optimum temperatures, but the consensus is that your room should be somewhere between 60 and 67°F. That is probably colder than what you're accustomed to. Sleeping too hot and sleeping too cold both have downsides, so find a temperature that works for you and track the differences in your sleep quality using a device like the Oura Ring. Fans and AC units are great ways to lower the temperature of your sleeping environment, and thermostats allow you to adjust for changes in room temperature.

Expected Health Benefit of Sleeping at Colder Temperatures:
• Deeper sleep

My Experience: Thankfully, I have always enjoyed sleeping in colder environments. When I met my wife, Rachel, I realized that some people take it a step further and enjoy sleeping in bedrooms that feel like the Arctic tundra. Overall, though, my research on sleep health always points to the benefits of sleeping in a colder bedroom, so unless I read otherwise, I will continue to enjoy the cold.

Pro Tip: Companies like Eight Sleep produce sleep systems and mattress pads that cool your mattress to a desired temperature. I use one of their products and I love it. The lowest setting on my system today is 55°F, the perfect temperature for me. The results on my Oura Ring have been spectacular.

> *"Keep your bedroom at 60 to 67°F (15 to 19°C) and think of your bedroom as your 'cave.' It should be cool, dark, and quiet to enhance your sleep."*[59]
> —Michelle Drerup, PsyD., director of behavioral sleep medicine at the Cleveland Clinic

Block Blue Light

Why: The sun's rays contain the full spectrum of colors, each emitting a different level of energy. Blue light is the strongest, and the one that helps you maintain a healthy circadian rhythm, rising with the sun and setting with the sun so that you can be energetic in the morning and sleepy in the evening. Unfortunately, phone screens, TV screens, and fluorescent lights all emit high levels of blue light as well, keeping you energized in their presence and affecting how long it takes you to fall asleep (sleep latency). When you consume blue light in the evening, scrolling on your phone or glued to the TV, you end up confusing your body by delaying the natural release of melatonin, which hurts your ability to sleep. Prolonged exposure to blue light throughout the day can also lead to eye strain, headaches, and eye degeneration.[60]

Expected Health Benefits of Blocking Blue Light:
- Improves sleep latency
- Improves overall sleep time
- Improves sleep efficiency
- Reduces sleep apnea
- Reduces impact on sleep cycles
- Reduces risk of eye disease

My Experience: I have noticed a big difference in my sleep quality by wearing blue light blocking glasses in the evenings. Most days, I follow the natural cycles of the sun by putting them on when the sun goes down and wearing them until I go to sleep. My favorite glasses are from TrueDark Eyewear.

Pro Tip: If you want to take this to the next level, look at the lighting you use in your home. Different lights emit different levels of blue light. For example, brushing your teeth in front of a fluorescent bulb might disrupt your evening at the last minute.

> *"Wear blue blocking glasses. This tip is especially important to do after sunset. Here's the kicker: not all blue blockers are made the same! You want to make sure that the blue blockers you're wearing after sunset block at least 95% of blue light."[61]*
> —Kelly Murray, founder of Kelly Murray Sleep Consulting

Test Hormones

Why: Hormones are chemicals in the body that act like messengers. After being produced in one part of the body, they travel to other parts where they help control how cells and organs perform their functions. Having too much or too little of certain hormones can negatively affect your well-being. This is called a hormone imbalance and can happen for a variety of reasons. By testing your hormones and comparing them to the average person your age, you can make adjustments to your lifestyle or take supplements to restore a natural hormone balance. Nowadays, there are companies that send you at-home testing kits enabling you to collect a sample of your blood, urine, or saliva and send it back for results. Some of the more common hormone tests measure your levels of estrogen and testosterone, as well as thyroid, pituitary gland, and adrenal gland function.

Expected Health Benefits of Testing Your Hormones (and restoring balance):
- The symptoms of a hormone imbalance can be wide-ranging and depend on the age and gender of each person. Some of the more common include weight gain, fatigue, muscle weakness, mood swings, loss of sex drive, and difficulty sleeping. By restoring balance, you can alleviate these problems.

My Experience: I originally purchased a Men's Health Test from Everlywell and was surprised to see my results. This data allowed me to make the right lifestyle changes to help restore my hormone balance.

Pro Tip: Your hormone levels change as you age, so I recommend testing them every couple of years and making the necessary lifestyle changes to stay balanced. I don't know much about hormone replacement or supplementation, but I do know some people who want to maintain the levels of testosterone they had in their 20s for the rest of their lives. Consult your doctor before making any changes.

> *"Biology is now an information technology, which means that the field of medicine is getting both better and cheaper at warp speed. Thanks to technology, every phase of medical treatment is being reimagined."*[62]
> —Tony Robbins and Peter Diamandis, co-authors of *Life Force*

Try Strange Foods

Why: When I was younger, I was scared to try new foods. I stuck to eating chicken and rice for most meals. Nowadays, I can't tell you how many times I have sat down at a restaurant and ordered the strangest thing on their menu, especially abroad. Our bodies and our guts are unique, so you never know what will make you feel like a superhero and what will cause you to run to the bathroom. I am willing to take that risk! As Aubrey Marcus outlines in his book, *Own the Day, Own Your Life*, "Lunch is an opportunity to reframe and restart your day. It's not an obligation to cross off the list. It's also an opportunity to get your body the micronutrients it needs to keep you feeling great. The way to do that isn't with something ordered off a cart. It's by experimenting and exploring."[63] This beautiful world is full of exotic plants, animals, and experiences. If you train yourself to be open to trying them, you never know what you'll find.

Expected Health Benefit of Eating a Weird Lunch:
- This one is hard to predict, and not always positive. Food has a major impact on how we feel and perform, both physically and cognitively. Trying new foods is fun, tasty, and sometimes very healthy.

My Experience: From svið (sheep head) and hákarl (fermented shark) in Iceland to rondón (Caribbean stew) in San Andrés, I have eaten some interesting meals. My wife and friends now expect me to order the strangest local cuisines when we travel, and we always have fun with it. Not only do some of these foods make it into my normal diet, but they also become good memories. You can become familiar with anything over time, especially adventurous eating.

Pro Tip: Our world today is obsessed with finding the next one-stop-shop superfood and I recommend trying whatever you can. Over the years, this curiosity has helped me try everything from sea moss gel to crickets.

> *"Without experimentation, a willingness to ask questions and try new things, we shall surely become static, repetitive, and moribund."*[64]
> —Anthony Bourdain, author of *World Travel*

Healthy Friends

Why: As you know, I believe you are the average of the five people you spend the most time with. So, if you spend more time with healthier people, you're inclined to become healthier yourself. The influence of these people is not always obvious, but it is consistent. Instead of sitting around gossiping, you'll find yourself talking about the latest health trends, athletic events to take part in, or new a superfood. These small differences in conversation will compound, leading you to a healthier lifestyle. If you can't find healthy friends, make them. Introduce your existing network to books like this and talk with them about the benefits of implementing these healthy habits. Help your friends see these habits through the positive and exciting lens that you do, and it will rub off on them.

My Experience: I grew up with a group of very competitive friends, for which I am grateful. Competition happens in many forms, and I find myself challenging my friends to compete with me in all sorts of ways. As I write, a handful of us are training for a half marathon. This has encouraged me to work harder at the gym, eat healthier, and focus on my flexibility. Healthy habits are always more fun and maintainable in a group setting.

Pro Tip: With whom do you spend the most time? For me, it's my wife. That means, mathematically, outside of myself, she has the biggest impact on my health. Getting her involved in the healthy habits mentioned throughout this chapter has helped me compound and reinforce the benefits of everything we do.

> *"The only mofos in my circle are people that I can learn from."*[65]
> —Questlove

Healthy Mentors

Why: Earlier in the book, we talked about a realization I had early in my personal development journey, which was that by reading a book, I was condensing decades of someone else's experience into mere days of self-education. Mentors don't have to meet with you in person—sometimes they mentor you through the books they've written. Personal experience is a great teacher, but other people's experiences are sometimes better.

By studying healthy people and the healthy habits they've put in place, you will find new concepts and activities to implement into your life. If you want to run a marathon, study some successful marathon runners and even ultra-marathon runners. If you want to bench 350lbs, study someone who has benched 500lbs. If you want to fast for 24 hours, read about someone who has fasted for 72 hours. By studying people who have done what you want to do and have done it well, you will realize what the human body is capable of, and it will encourage you to push your health boundaries even further.

My Experience: When I was in high school and college, I wanted to learn from my own experiences. I rarely consulted my friends or family about diet and exercise. After reading some books on healthy living, however, it quickly became one of my favorite genres. None of the healthy habits in this chapter are things I originally thought of. They all came from the experience and research of the amazing men and women who have written the books I have read. I will continue studying these healthy people for the rest of my life.

Pro Tip: These healthy mentors are easier to reach than you think. After running a personal development podcast for the last few years, I have been able to interview some of my favorite healthy mentors and apply those conversations to my own development journey. These authors are usually driven by a purpose to help their communities become healthier. By asking them great questions, you'll often get great responses.

> *"A mentor is someone who sees more talent and ability within you, than you see in yourself, and helps bring it out of you."*[66]
> —Bob Proctor, author of *You Were Born Rich*

Follow Healthy People

Why: In the same way that you become the average of the five people you spend the most time with, you also become the average of your social media feed. If your feed is full of unhealthy behavior, it will negatively impact your health. If your feed is full of healthy behavior, it will positively impact your health. Your subconscious is always consuming information, so make it overwhelmingly healthy information, especially if you're spending a good amount of time scrolling on social media. I love reading books, but I have also found some valuable information by following healthy people. Social media is a great platform for healthy authors to communicate with their followers and share content from their books that their readers are looking for.

My Experience: I first became aware of the unhealthy content on my Instagram feed after college. I was following a bunch of party type accounts that encouraged me to drink more alcohol and a bunch of hustle type accounts that encouraged me to work more than sleep. By consciously going through my feed and removing the negative accounts, I was heading in the right direction. After that, I started adding healthy authors' accounts to my page and gradually, the algorithm changed in my favor. These small but subtle changes in your life will compound and have much larger impacts over time.

Pro Tip: Survey your healthiest friends and ask which accounts they follow for health-related tips. You'll be surprised how many accounts exist that you'd never stumble upon, yourself.

> *"A healthy man wants a thousand things; a sick man only wants one."*[67]
>
> —Confucius, Chinese philosopher

Wealthy Habits

Cut Unhealthy Spending

Why: You've probably heard there are only two ways to become rich: spend less or earn more. Well, one of the best ways to spend less is to cut unhealthy spending on unhealthy habits, such as cigarettes, alcohol, junk food, and sugary $8 coffees. It all compounds. For example, an $8 sugary drink every day for a year adds up to roughly $3,000 and a whole heck of unnecessary calories. Can you believe that number? Not only can you save $3,000 a year and lose some weight by cutting back on that one unhealthy habit, but that money has an opportunity cost.

What if you invested that money instead of spending it? By cutting unhealthy spending, you're becoming healthier and wealthier, killing two birds with one stone. I recommend having an honest look through your bank statements and seeing how much you may be able to save.

My Experience: I was shocked when I realized how much money I was actively spending on unhealthy habits. After college, I continued eating unhealthy fast foods and spending way too much money on alcohol. Driven primarily by a motivation to feel better and have more energy, I stopped this unhealthy habit and started saving more. It felt great, both health-wise and financially.

Pro Tip: If some of your unhealthy spending habits bring a lot of joy to your life, I recommend doing an 80/20-style inventory. List all the unhealthy habits you're currently spending money on and give them a happiness rating from 0-10. Then, cut your spending on all the unhealthy habits that aren't driving significant levels of happiness (rated below 8) and keep spending on the ones that do. Normally, this means you'll be able to cut 80% of your spending because it only drives 20% of your happiness.

> *"Spend extravagantly on the things you love, and cut costs mercilessly on the things you don't."*[68]
>
> —Ramit Sethi, author of *I Will Teach You To Be Rich*

Cut Unhappy Spending

Why: Unhappy spending simply means spending money on unhappy habits. An example is paying subscriptions fees to streaming services. These programs might give you a short burst of dopamine, but they often leave you feeling as though you could have done more with your time. They encourage procrastination. The money you're spending on these unhappy habits adds up and compounds. For example, $15 a month on Netflix plus two hours a night of consumption adds up to $180 a year and over 700 hours of viewing time. What is the opportunity cost of those 700 hours? A fully functioning side hustle? A new language? A new skill set? By cutting unhappy spending habits, you're becoming both happier and wealthier.

My Experience: Would you rather suffer the pain of discipline or the pain of regret? Sometimes, these unhappy spending habits are disguised as happy ones. Think about the long-term impact of the money you're spending and see if any of those habits you're funding are leaving you worse off in the long run. I was able to find a handful of these and cut them off, saving me money and time.

Pro Tip: If some of your unhappy spending habits are still helping you become healthier, try doing an 80/20-style inventory as described above. List all the unhappy habits you're currently spending money on and give them a health rating from 0-10. Then cut your spending on all those habits that aren't driving significant levels of health (rated below eight) and keep spending on the ones that do. Normally, this means you'll be able to cut 80% of your spending because it only drives 20% of the health benefits. An example of this could be a workout subscription you rarely use.

> *"We buy things we don't need with money we don't have to impress people we don't like."*[69]
>
> —Dave Ramsey, author of *The Total Money Makeover*

Set a Savings Goal

Why: I have never been a big fan of the term "budgeting." Why? It feels constricting and takes the fun out of financial planning. Instead of budgeting for how much you can spend in different areas of your life, I recommend setting an annual savings goal. Then take that goal and break it down into a weekly or monthly amount and set up an automated transfer with your bank to withdraw the money and put it into a separate savings account based on your goals. Everything left over is free to spend, because you know you're actively contributing to your annual savings goal. Micromanaging a budget works for some people, but not everyone.

My Experience: I have been operating this way for years now. Instead of stressing over each dollar I spend, I prefer to set an annual savings goal, automate it, and then do high-level audits from time to time. By working this way, I don't have to worry about spending too much on food or leisure. If the money is there, it can be spent however my heart desires because I know I am still on target to hit my savings goal. By performing audits from time to time on any unhealthy or unhappy spending, I am always optimizing the way I spend my money. This leaves me feeling happy and removes the micromanagement of money from my mind.

Pro Tip: Set up a separate bank account for your savings. I do all my banking on my phone through a series of mobile apps. I set up the automated transfer of my monthly savings goal from my checking account (where I am paid) to my savings account (where I save) and then deleted the savings account app from my phone, so I wouldn't be tempted to access it. Now, my savings fund is steadily building, and I don't feel the need to check it all the time. Out of sight, out of mind.

> *"Do not save what is left after spending, but spend what is left after saving."*[70]
>
> —Warren Buffett, CEO of Berkshire Hathaway

Set Up an Emergency Fund

Why: An emergency fund, also known as a contingency fund, is a bank account with money set aside as a financial safety net. It is used to pay for large, unexpected expenses, such as unforeseen medical bills, home or car repairs, or sudden unemployment. The idea here is that no matter what, you won't be thrown into financial chaos. This stability adds a sense of security and gives you a solid foundation to operate from, especially when taking risks. Just as for your savings goals, I recommend opening a separate savings account and setting up an automated transfer from your checking account. This way, the account will continue to grow while you'll be insulated from unexpected expenses. How much should you save? Well, as a rule of thumb, set aside at least six months of fixed expenses. I know that sounds like a lot at first, but you can save up to that amount over the course of the next couple of years if necessary.

My Experience: Thankfully, I was introduced to this concept in one of the first books I read, and I immediately put it into action. I transferred a few thousand dollars from my checking account into a separate savings account, set up an automated transfer from my checking account, and then deleted the app from my phone. I didn't even notice the weekly transfer, which was great. Now, years later, I am insulated from financial disaster. I hope I never have to use it.

Pro Tip: An emergency fund must be liquid enough to be used in an emergency, but that doesn't mean it should just sit there. I try to invest both my savings and my emergency fund in low-risk, liquefiable investment vehicles so that as they protect me and give me peace of mind, they also earn me money. Do some research and find an option that works for you. Remember, the purpose of an emergency fund is not to make you money, so please don't get risky with it.

> *"Planning is important, but the most important part of every plan is to plan on the plan not going according to plan."*[71]
> —Morgan Housel, author of *The Psychology of Money*

Use Financial Tracking Software

Why: Do you know what your net worth is? How about how much cash you have available or what your outstanding credit is? All these questions can be easily answered by implementing a personal financial tracking application. These tools integrate with all your financial accounts, such as your checking, savings, investment, and credit accounts. Daily, they aggregate your data across your portfolio and present it to you in a variety of ways, all in one place. Plenty of different trackers are available and each has a different core focus; for example, budgeting or investing. Remember: it's hard to manage what you don't measure. Some of the major players in the space are Quicken, Mint, YNAB, TurboTax, Tiller Money, FutureAdvisor, and Mvelopes. Try them all and see what works best for you.

My Experience: I was finally motivated to implement some financial tracking software after reading *I Will Teach You To Be Rich* by Ramit Sethi. After a quick analysis of my options, I chose a software called Personal Capital. Within 30 minutes, I was able to fully integrate around 10 different financial accounts and see my overall financial situation for the first time. The tool also allows me to view trends in my spending, investing, and more.

Pro Tip: Each of these tools has an auto-email function, so you can receive snapshots of your financial picture on a daily or weekly basis without having to log in every day. I have mine set to deliver weekly, which gives me enough data to ensure I am hitting my goals. I love these tools!

> *"What's measured improves."*[72]
>
> —Peter Drucker, author of *Managing Oneself*

Protect Your Credit Score

Why: Many countries have their own credit scoring systems, but in this wealthy habit I will be focusing on the United States. A credit score depicts a consumer's creditworthiness, also known as your likelihood of paying a loan back on time. These scores are sourced from credit bureaus, which are organizations that collect massive amounts of credit information. Since these scores determine the probability of paying back borrowed money, they are reviewed by lenders any time you apply to borrow money. I recommend downloading a free credit score application like Credit Karma to regularly monitor your credit score and the factors contributing to it. Some of these include payment history, credit card use, derogatory marks, credit age, total number of accounts, and hard inquiries. Once you understand these variables, you can monitor them and protect them from lowering. Tools like these also have articles on repairing credit, building credit, and understanding each variable in more detail.

My Experience: I have been using Credit Karma to monitor my credit since I was in college. This free tool has helped me keep track of my credit worthiness and as a result, I never had to worry about getting approved for loans. For example, I was able to invest in multiple multi-family rental properties because I protected my credit score.

Pro Tip: If you're worried about your credit score, there are many online programs and companies dedicated to repairing it. Although it seems somewhat arbitrary at times, you never need a solid credit score until you need a solid credit score. If you're reading this and have no idea what your score is, I advise you check it out.

> *"In times past, your social security number was the most influential number known to man... However, there is a three-digit number that is giving the social security number a run for its money..."*[73]
> —Cornelius J., author of *The Credit Repair Book*

Think Bigger

Why: In a world of limitless possibilities, why do so many people live under their potential? Especially financially? People say money is the root of all evil, but I disagree. I think money amplifies who you already are. A great person can do so much more with money than they can without it. If your impact is determined by how many people you serve and how well you serve them, money can accelerate your impact. One of the best ways to become wealthy then, is to start thinking bigger. Small thinking is the same as arguing for limiting beliefs. If you argue for your limiting beliefs, you get to keep them. One of my favorite ways to reprogram my thinking is to stop whatever task I'm doing and ask myself, "What would it look like to do this 10 times bigger?" Sometimes, simply sitting in that headspace for a minute or so will create bigger ideas I can apply to the task at hand. If your goal is to earn $250,000 next year, spend some time thinking about what it would take to earn $2,500,000. Is the goal attainable? Probably not. But the thought exercise could lead to a creative way to earn more than you initially expected and crush your baseline goal.

My Experience: After reading a few books about thinking bigger, I realized that the most important discoveries I made happened when I took just a few minutes each day to deliberately think bigger. It's a fun exercise and has absolutely created more wealth for me. One specific example came when I thought about how I could multiply the average deal size for my author promotion business tenfold. Did I manage it? No, but in a matter of days, I had doubled it. I had been unaware of the potential because I was thinking small.

Pro Tip: Thinking bigger can be toxic if done incorrectly. Sometimes, practitioners set unrealistic expectations and then hold themselves accountable to those unrealistic expectations. The thought experiments are fun, but always run through your SMARTI framework before putting a new goal into practice.

> *"Success is determined not so much by the size of one's brain as it is by the size of one's thinking."*[74]
>
> —David Schwartz, author of *The Magic of Thinking Big*

Install Play Bigger Triggers

Why: In Chapter 2, I outlined the importance of installing environmental cues such as motivational posters or desk ornaments to help train your subconscious mind to default to a certain thought pattern. I call them "Play Bigger Triggers," or PBTs, because if used correctly, they positively influence you to grow. You can set their intention to anything you'd like, including health-, wealth-, or happiness-related goals. Can you think of any PBTs you can install in your work environment that would subconsciously encourage you to become wealthier? If you work at a computer, one of the best examples is hanging some wealth-related art on the walls behind your monitor. That way, even when you're not focused on them, the motivational messages are always within your peripheral vision. Maybe place some motivational ornaments on your desk or sticky notes on your bathroom mirror. Motivational T-shirts and tattoos count too. (Ha-ha.)

My Experience: When I first learned about this concept, I bought five T-shirts that said "Think Big" across the chest and decided to cycle through them for an entire month. Can you guess what happened that month? Each time an opportunity presented itself to me, I started thinking bigger. Now, I try to implement PBTs in every area of my life. Why not?

Pro Tip: If you're looking for high-quality motivational canvas art to hang in your workspace, I recommend checking out Ikonick. I have a few pieces hanging in my office and I have subconsciously absorbed their messages tens of thousands of times.

> "My teacher Jim Rohn taught me a simple principle: every day, stand guard at the door of your mind, and you alone decide what thoughts and beliefs you let into your life. For they will shape whether you feel rich or poor, cursed or blessed."[75]
>
> —Tony Robbins, author of MONEY *Master the Game*

Think 80/20

Why: In 1906, Italian economist and civil engineer Vilfredo Pareto noticed that 20% of the pea pods in his garden were generating 80% of the peas. Curious, Pareto then analyzed Italy's income distribution and found that 20% of the population was generating 80% of the income.[76] This analysis is now commonly referred to as The 80/20 Rule, The Pareto Principle, The Law of the Vital Few, or The Principle of Factor Sparsity and applies to many areas of life, not just peas and income distribution.

I have personally found that in most life circumstances, 20% of the effort generates 80% of the impact. This has allowed me to categorize activities as highly leveraged and poorly leveraged. In each life circumstance, you want to do more of the highly leveraged activities and fewer poorly leveraged ones. For example, in sales, most of the time, 20% of your prospecting activities will lead to 80% of your sales. The goal? Do more of that 20% and, as Tim Ferriss suggests, automate, eliminate, or delegate the rest. The result? More sales in less time. It's fascinating! So, my questions to you are, "What is the 20% of activity in your life that is leading to 80% of your income?" Then, within that activity, which 20% of that activity is leading to 80% of the success? You can go down multiple levels in this line of questioning until you find the highest-leveraged activity in your life. That is how thinking 80/20 can help you improve your wealth.

My Experience: After discovering the 80/20 Rule in *The 4-Hour Workweek* by Tim Ferriss, I applied the rule to my sales job. I was quickly able to analyze my outbound sales activity and I discovered a certain type of prospect that was generating most of my sales. Instead of wasting my time on prospects that did not fit the criteria, I was able to work less and generate more.

Pro Tip: If you choose not to run an 80/20 analysis on your work and you continue to put your time into poorly leveraged activities, you're living under your potential. If you're working within a role where you can't ignore the 80% of activity that only leads to 20% of the results, try hiring a virtual assistant. Just because certain work is not fulfilling to you does not mean it won't be fulfilling to someone else. Fulfillment is relative.

> *"Remember that if you don't prioritize your life, someone else will."*[77]
> —Greg McKeown, author of *Essentialism*

Trick Parkinson's Law

Why: In 1957, British naval historian C. Northcote Parkinson published a book titled *Parkinson's Law*, which introduced the concept that "work expands so as to fill the time available for its completion." This concept is now referred to as Parkinson's Law[78], but by tricking it, you can use its premise to skyrocket your productivity and limit your spending. Here's how. From a productivity standpoint, the most common example of this law can be found in the classroom. As a student, how many times growing up were you assigned a multi-week project and you found yourself completing it the night before it was due, in just a few hours? You could have completed everything on the night it was assigned, but because of Parkinson's Law, you expanded the work to fill the time available. To boost your productivity, reverse engineer this law and start giving yourself shorter timelines for completion on large projects. The quality of your work will not suffer, and you'll start getting more done.

From a spending standpoint, we could rewrite the rule to say, "Spending expands to fill the amount available in your bank account." Funny, right? Not so much. Therefore, as we start to make more money in our lives, it always seems to disappear. Our spending adjusts accordingly, and magically, we are no better off with a raise at work than we were without it. Again, reverse engineer Parkinson's Law and set an expense goal that is slightly less than you're used to. You can start small, by reducing your spending in the next month by as little as 5%. What you'll probably notice is that you adjusted your spending to fit this new threshold, not even noticing that it was less than the previous month. Thank you, Parkinson!

My Experience: This law seriously works like magic. From a productivity perspective, I used to find myself assigning long timelines for projects I assumed to be difficult. What happened? They took the full timeline. By hacking this and consciously shortening the timelines of my projects, now I get a lot more done in less time.

Pro Tip: As for spending, start transferring money to a separate account, maybe even at a different bank, so that you're not tempted to touch it. You will quickly adjust to the new amount of available funds and naturally start spending less money. It works like a charm.

> *"Profit is not an event. It's a habit."*[79]
>
> —Mike Michalowicz, author of *Profit First*

Use Six Thinking Hats

Why: In 1985, Maltese author and psychologist Edward de Bono published a book titled *Six Thinking Hats*, which outlines a decision-making process that allows an individual or group of people to investigate a problem from a variety of perspectives. It teaches you how to separate your thinking into six different functions. By mentally wearing and switching "hats," you and your team can focus or redirect thoughts, one at a time. For example, while wearing the white hat, a participant can only present facts. Then, they might put on the yellow hat and analyze the problem from an optimistic point of view, describing the positives they see with the problem at hand. To balance it out, you might then put on the black hat and discuss the risks, challenges, or difficulties you see. What's the outcome? Clear, organized decision-making. How does the concept of six thinking hats relate to wealth? Well, wealthy decision-making can be extremely complex and sometimes very emotional, especially in a group setting. By using this framework to analyze your decision-making, you can be much clearer, objective, and more aligned.

My Experience: A mentor of mine, grandmaster Kevin Horsley, originally introduced this framework to me. After walking through each hat with Kevin, I started to see situations from different perspectives and was able to make better decisions. I have been using this framework, individually and in a group setting, to work my way through almost every major problem I face.

Pro Tip: If you choose to implement this framework in a group setting, I have found that designating a mediator or facilitator works well. This person is there to keep the conversation on track and bring participants back to the "hat" they're wearing, advance the conversation, and take notes. Otherwise, conversations can quickly bounce from hat to hat and spiral out of control.

> *"A discussion should be a genuine attempt to explore a subject rather than a battle between competing egos."*[80]
> —Edward de Bono, author of *Six Thinking Hats*

Lock Up Your Phone

Why: The average American spends over five hours per day on their phone, picking it up an average of 96 separate times, which works out to about once every ten minutes.[81] What a distraction! How are we supposed to get quality work done when we are checking our devices that often? Tim Ferriss and James Clear talked about the benefits of locking up their phones on a recent podcast using a locking container called Kitchen Safe.[82] The box is large enough to hold a few phones and has a built-in timer, allowing you to lock up your device during a period of deep work. Author Nir Eyal calls this type of technique a "precommitment," meaning you're choosing to remove the future choice of picking up your device when it pings by putting it in a lock box.[83] By removing your device from your immediate view and making it more difficult to access, you'll be free to focus on what matters most.

My Experience: This box has been a game-changer for me. Although I am fully aware of how distracting my device can be and have most notifications turned off, I still find myself mindlessly scrolling social platforms during the workday. These platforms are addictive! By locking up my phone for hours at a time, I have been able to focus much more effortlessly. This habit pairs well with the Pomodoro Technique mentioned next.

Pro Tip: If you want to spend more quality time with your family, make it a rule that everyone puts their devices in the lock box during dinner time. This way, no one at the table can be distracted by their phones, giving everyone the chance to be more present. Although I don't have children yet, I know this will be a family practice in the future.

> *"Every action you take is a vote for the type of person you wish to become. No single instance will transform your beliefs, but as the votes build up, so does the evidence of your new identity."*[84]
> —James Clear, author of *Atomic Habits*

Use the Pomodoro Technique

Why: In the late 1980s, entrepreneur and author Francesco Cirillo invented a time management system called the Pomodoro Technique, in which you break your work into intervals, traditionally of 25 minutes each, separated by breaks. The idea is that we work better in sprints than we do in marathons. Each interval of work is known as a pomodoro, which comes from the Italian word for tomato, after Cirillo discovered the technique by using a small tomato-shaped kitchen timer. The technique has six simple steps. First, decide on the task. Next, set the timer to 25 minutes. Third, work on the task at hand. Once the timer rings, you take a short break, typically five to 10 minutes. The fifth step is to repeat the process until you've gone through three pomodoros. The sixth and final step is to take a longer break after your fourth pomodoro, so that you can recharge and get ready to start all over again. You'd be surprised at how efficiently this technique works.

My Experience: I initially had some trouble implementing this one. I had trained myself to work for long periods of time without an interruption, so it felt unnatural to take breaks after such a "short" interval. But with practice, it started to feel more natural and now, I can absolutely see the benefits of working this way. Looking at tasks through the lens of Parkinson's Law, you can see how condensing your day's tasks into short 25-minute bursts is a great way to get a lot of work done. In fact, I am using this technique to work my way through the writing process of this book.

Pro Tip: By purchasing a small red tomato kitchen timer and using it to measure your pomodoro sprints, you're taking advantage of the Play Bigger Trigger idea. These items are cheap and can be found from most major retailers, such as Amazon. By using the same device that Cirillo did when he discovered the technique, I feel aligned with it and motivated to continue using it. Be sure to set your phone to silent—or put it in your lock box—and let your coworkers know it's pomodoro time if they try to grab your attention!

> *"If you want to make something hard, indeed truly impossible, to complete, all you have to do is make the end goal as vague as possible."*[85]
>
> —Greg McKeown, author of *Essentialism*

Eat a Frog Every Workday

Why: There is an old saying that if the first thing you do each morning is eat a big live frog, you'll spend the rest of the day knowing you're done with the worst thing you'll have to do that day. It's a freeing feeling, whereas if you decided to procrastinate and put off the frog-eating until the evening, you'd be distracted all day, knowing you must still eat a frog. In Brian Tracy's best-selling book, *Eat That Frog!* he shows us that we can leverage this adage to increase our productivity. Successful people focus on their most important tasks first and get them done. That way, they can spend the rest of the day knowing that nothing will stand in their way. Tracy teaches his readers how to structure their mornings using decision, discipline, and determination. In a world full of distraction, this framework will allow you to accomplish more each morning than most people do all day.

My Experience: This practice was very easy to adopt. Since I had already been prioritizing my tasks based on leverage (80/20), I knew I needed to move those tasks to the morning. Coincidentally, workday mornings right after a good workout are when I usually have the most energy, so working on my most important tasks then is a great improvement as opposed to at the end of the day when my energy is lower.

Pro Tip: If you work out of a calendar like I do, block off your mornings for eating frogs. This way, no one can book time on my calendar while I am focused on getting my most important work done. You'll hear my pomodoro timer going off every 25 minutes each morning as I work through my frogs!

> *"If you have to eat two frogs, eat the ugliest one first."*[86]
> —Brian Tracy, author of *Eat That Frog!*

Bookend Your Workdays

Why: Bookends support the end of a row of books to keep them from falling over and often come in pairs. Have you ever thought about bookending your days by implementing a solid morning routine and a solid evening routine? If you can control the start of your day and the end of your day, you have a much better chance of keeping the middle of your day from falling apart. Just like physical bookends, your routines can come in a variety of shapes and sizes. Which bookend is more important? Your morning routine. Why? It sets the tone for your day. In the same way that making your bed projects you into the rest of your day with a small win, a solid morning routine can project you into your day with a bunch of small wins, ready to eat a frog. Earlier in the book, we talked about bookending your day by reading for 15 minutes in the morning and 15 minutes in the evening. This is a great place to start!

My Experience: I had always known the importance of having a morning routine, but I never took it seriously until I read *The Miracle Morning* by Hal Elrod. Hal teaches his readers a six-step morning routine framework I implemented for myself—it changed my life. He encourages his readers to practice silence, affirmations, visualization, exercise, reading, and scribing (journaling). My morning routines are quite a bit longer than my evening routines, but they are both incredibly important to me.

Pro Tip: Evening routines can be very powerful as well. I have read that your last thought before bed is usually your first thought after waking up. You want to make it count. If you only put a bookend on one side of your book collection, they'll start falling off the other side. Balance both ends.

"Discipline creates lifestyle."[87]

—Hal Elrod, author of *The Miracle Morning*

Location, Location, Location

Why: Where you choose to live matters less today than it did a few years ago, but it still matters more than you might think. Not only can you save money by moving to an area where real estate is less expensive, but in the United States, different states have different income taxes. For example, as I am writing this, Florida and Texas have 0% income tax, whereas California and New Jersey have income taxes over 10%. That is a massive difference over a lifetime of income. Although it's hard to measure, where you live also has a major impact on your earning potential. Certain cities, like Austin, San Francisco, and Boston are growing and considered tech hubs, whereas other cities, like Detroit, Youngstown, and Cleveland have experienced major declines in financial opportunity. If you're around massive earning potential all the time, just like the 'five friends' adage, you'll be more likely to find opportunities to earn.

My Experience: When I first read about the importance of location from a financial perspective, I was shocked. Why doesn't everyone think of things through this lens? So, after some long discussions with friends and family, I decided to relocate. Doesn't it sound nice to spend less, earn more, get more space, and be closer to financial opportunities? I know it sounds great to me. Florida, here I come!

Pro Tip: For remote workers, it's becoming more popular to consider relocating to offices in international cities. Oftentimes for US citizens, many major Latin American cities are far less expensive than their US counterparts. I would encourage anyone to spend a month or two in cities like Medellín, Buenos Aires, or Panama City because of the warm weather and great exchange rates.

> *"Every location has its own cost of living. The cost of living is the amount of money you need to maintain your standard of living in a given location. Rent/mortgage, food, transportation, clothing, entertainment, equipment, education, and taxes are just some of the basic expenses that can fluctuate from place to place."*[88]
> —Jim Miller, author of *Budgeting Doesn't Have to Suck*

Eat Smarter

Why: In the same vein as cutting unhealthy spending habits, eating smarter can also improve your productivity and earning potential. You know the feeling of having eaten something that makes you feel bloated, tired, and nauseous? Try eating those bad foods and then performing at your best in any professional capacity. It won't happen. Then there are middle-of-the-road foods that leave you feeling normal. They won't negatively impact your productivity or earning potential, but they won't help accelerate them either. On the other hand, there are foods that are scientifically proven to help us maximize our cognitive performance. For example, in Jim Kwik's book, *Limitless*, he outlines "The Top 10 Brain Foods:" avocados, blueberries, broccoli, dark chocolate, eggs, green leafy vegetables, salmon/sardines/caviar, turmeric, walnuts, and water. Consuming foods like these on a regular basis will enable you to perform at a higher level, allowing you to improve your productivity and earning potential. Plus, when considering the health costs associated with eating poor-quality foods, eating healthier kinds can be less expensive than junk food, saving you money in the long run.

My Experience: This coincides with many of the Healthy Habits I listed in the previous chapter, but I have been eating intentionally for a handful of years now. By eliminating foods that make me feel unproductive and doubling down on foods that improve my productivity, I feel great...all the time.

Pro Tip: Have you heard of nootropics? They are basically smart drugs that boost your cognitive performance. Some of them are natural, whereas others are lab-created. I consider the foods listed above, the brain foods, to be natural nootropics. They work just like these other synthetic substances to improve your output. What you put into your body makes a big difference in what comes out of your mind and mouth. If you're not eating this way, you're choosing to live under your full potential.

> *"Our most precious gift is our brain. It is what allows us to learn, love, think, create, and even to experience joy. It is the gateway to our emotions, to our capacity for deeply experiencing life, to our ability to have lasting intimacy. It allows us to innovate, grow, and accomplish."*[89]
>
> —Jim Kwik, author of *Limitless*

Start a Side Hustle

Why: A side hustle is any type of employment undertaken in addition to your full-time job. People start side hustles to earn additional income, learn additional skills, and take control of their lives by adopting an entrepreneurial mindset. Side hustles don't have to be entrepreneurial in nature, but most of the time, they are. For example, if you're working as a full-time copywriter, you might do freelance copywriting after hours. In this scenario, not only are you starting to learn the basics of entrepreneurship, sales, marketing, client acquisition, client management, and customer service, but you're also making money in the process. As someone who values skill acquisition above almost anything else, I think everyone should have a side hustle related to their passion or chosen industry. Side hustles can also be part-time jobs or internships where you can try out a new line of work or build your skills in another discipline. One of the major benefits of side hustles is that you don't have to rely on them for income, which means you can take them at your own pace and really enjoy the process.

My Experience: My first business, BookThinkers, started as a side hustle. For years, I worked on building the business after normal working hours. I joked that my software job was my nine-to-five and BookThinkers was my five-to-nine. While building the business, I was learning new skills I could apply to my full-time job and vice versa. Eventually, the per-hour income ratios started to reverse themselves and the hours I was spending on my "side hustle" became more valuable than the hours I was spending on my full-time job. Side hustles don't have to replace your full-time job, but if you're looking to become an entrepreneur, starting a side hustle is a great way to start.

Pro Tip: Ask yourself, "If money were no object, what would I spend my time doing?" If something pops into your head immediately but does not align with your full-time job, starting a side hustle is the best way to start working toward your dream life. Slow and steady wins the race. The best time to plant a tree was 20 years ago, right? You might as well start working toward your dreams today.

> *"Never despise small beginnings, and don't belittle your own accomplishments. Remember them and use them as inspiration as you go on to the next thing. When you venture outside your comfort zone, wherever the starting point may be, it's kind of a big deal."*[90]
> —Chris Guillebeau, author of *The $100 Startup*

Turn Your Car into a Mobile University

Why: According to a new survey from the AAA Foundation or Traffic Safety, American drivers spend an average of 293 hours behind the wheel every year.[91] What do most people do when they get into their car alone? Well, if they're like me, they put on their favorite music and sing their hearts out. Although I fully support this, it shouldn't be the only thing you do in the car. I recommend turning your car into a mobile university by listening to audiobooks, at least sometimes. When I'm on the road, listening to audiobooks is my favorite way to pass the time while learning something new. I try to remind myself that listening to the same song 500 times doesn't have any advantages, whereas listening to the right audiobook might completely change my life.

My Experience: Over time, I have realized that I prefer listening to biographies, autobiographies, or fiction in the car because these genres tend to have fewer note-taking opportunities and are more visual to listen to. I have gone on many long, multi-day road trips where we spend most of our day listening to audiobooks, including a recent trip where we drove an extra four hours on the first leg of the trip because we didn't want to shut the book off.

Pro Tip: Some of my favorite audiobooks are *Can't Hurt Me* by David Goggins, *Will* by Will Smith, *Greenlights* by Matthew McConaughey, *Beyond Order* by Jordan Peterson, *Sapiens* by Yuval Noah Harrari, *Steve Jobs* by Walter Isaacson, and *Living with a Seal* by Jesse Itzler.

> *"Accept responsibility for your life. Know that it is you who will get you where you want to go, no one else."*[92]
> —Les Brown, author of *You've Got To Be Hungry*

Build Your Personal Brand

Why: Your personal brand is the way you promote yourself to the outside world. Since the most important currency moving forward is attention, personal brands are going to become more important than ever as the world continues to evolve digitally. A few years ago, when you wanted to know about someone, you typed their name into a search engine and skimmed through the results. Today, you look them up on social media. These social platforms, especially Instagram, have become their own search engines. You can either curate your content and define what people see when they land on your profile, or you can let them make their own judgments. Ask yourself, "Who do I want to be and for what do I want to be known?" Then follow it up with, "Does my personal brand clearly communicate that today?" If not, get to work. Personal branding is important for professional networking and developing business relationships, and I think of it in the same way I think of side hustles. In fact, starting and managing your own personal brand can quickly become a source of supplemental income if desired.

My Experience: As someone who struggled with social media early on, I was not a fan of starting a personal brand at first. Then, as my business profiles started to grow and I began to understand the importance of social media, personal branding grew on me. Now, I pay very close attention to what I'm posting and how other people perceive my content. You never know who's watching.

Pro Tip: As I recommended in the Side Hustle section, ask yourself, "If money were no object, what would I spend my time doing?" Then, start building a personal brand that feeds that type of lifestyle. I don't recommend the whole 'fake it 'til you make it' type of social media feed, but if you want to be a full-time travel blogger, for example, stop posting pictures of yourself in your cubicle.

> *"Absorb what is useful, discard what is useless, and add what is specifically your own."*[93]
>
> —Bruce Lee, martial artist, actor, director, and philosopher

Borrow Credibility

Why: Whether you're building a personal or business brand, or working for someone else, one of the fastest ways to grow your online presence, leapfrog your competition, and make a name for yourself is to borrow credibility. The idea here is to work with the most trusted individuals and businesses in your industry and *to be seen* working with them. Credibility is very important—it will improve the likelihood of your next prospect doing business with you—but it is also hard to build by yourself and takes a huge amount of time and effort. Instead, by working with people who have already established credibility for themselves, you can fast forward and reach your goals much more quickly. This works because trust is transitive. You might not trust me yet, but I am pictured with your favorite business icon, so you're now instantly much more likely to trust me. The result? You're more likely to follow me or buy my products or services.

My Experience: I implemented this concept by starting a podcast. Each week, I would interview one of the world's top authors and in exchange for their time, I would help them market and sell their books. It was win-win. Then, on my socials, I could repost the content and be seen talking with people who had far more credibility than I. The result was amazing. My following grew much faster and my prospects were much more likely to do business with me.

Pro Tip: Reaching hard to reach people is an art form. There should be entire books dedicated to this subject. If you're looking to implement this one, I would recommend reading *The Third Door* by Alex Banayan and *Bluefishing* by Steve Sims. Together, these books have given me the frameworks I needed to reach some of the world's hardest to reach people.

> *"The best negotiating tactic is to build a genuine, trusting relationship. If you're an unknown entrepreneur and the person you're dealing with isn't invested in you, why would he or she even do business with you? On the other hand, if the person is your mentor or friend, you might not even need to negotiate."*[94]
>
> —Alex Banayan, author of *The Third Door*

Use a CRM

Why: Quick story. A while back, I reached out to one of my favorite authors and met him for coffee. It was an amazing experience, and he asked a lot of questions about me and my personal life. Years later, I invited him onto my podcast and before we hit record, it was almost as if we had been sipping coffee together just the day before. He followed up on names and situations I had shared with him years prior, without missing a beat. I asked him how he was able to remember those details because it truly made me feel special. He revealed that he uses a CRM, a customer relationship management software, to record the specifics of his conversations. That way, he can simply look up the details of his last chat before he meets with someone again. Genius. If you want to develop an amazing network and be known as someone who truly cares about the people they interact with, implement a CRM software, and get organized. People do business with people they like, and this is a great way to be liked.

My Experience: I started using Salesforce, one of the most recognizable sales CRMs, back in 2015 during a sales internship. I have been using it ever since. From a personal relationship management standpoint, it has allowed me to make everyone feel special and it shows that I am someone they can rely on to listen, take notes, stay organized, and follow through on promises. Nothing slips through the cracks. I have been playing around with a new CRM tool called Less Annoying CRM and have been enjoying that too.

Pro Tip: Our memories fade fast, so I recommend taking notes immediately after you finish a conversation, especially if you're at a networking event or conference where you're meeting a lot of people. Most platforms have easy-to-use mobile functionality so you can get some quick notes into a profile no matter where you are. You can also check notes at the drop of a hat prior to your next meeting with someone. Mentioning their kids' names, hobbies, or an inside joke they told you years before helps to build trust and rapport.

> *"Your income is determined by how many people you serve and how well you serve them."*[95]
>
> —Bob Burg and John David Mann, co-authors of *The Go-Giver*

Make Your Word Your Bond

Why: When someone's word is their bond, it means they always keep their promises. As you level up in life and start working with credible people, you'll want to keep those relationships healthy, so integrity is imperative. You want to show people that you mean business and can be trusted—if you say something will get done, get it done. Be careful here, because it takes years to build credibility but only a moment to destroy it. A mistake young professionals often make is over-promising and then under-delivering. They want to catch the attention of the bigwigs in the room, so they overstate their existing credibility or ability to execute something. Then, when they come up empty-handed, they've ruined their opportunity to develop valuable relationships. Only promise what you can deliver. Tell the truth and be transparent.

My Experience: Unfortunately, I have seen many people make mistakes in this area over the years. One day you're riding high, and the next, you break your promise to someone, and the ripple effects are huge. Think of celebrities or politicians who have lived a decent life, until one mistake brings down their empire and the world no longer trusts them. That is how business works too. It's far easier to live just one version of reality—the truth. That way, you don't have to filter through the different storylines and sets of promises you've made. Keep it straight. Keep it clean.

Pro Tip: As a socially active person, it's not uncommon for me to meet a dozen or more people in a day, either in person or on social media. That potentially leads to a lot of promises being made. To keep those promises and my follow-ups organized, I've implemented CRM software as we discussed in the last habit. This is a lifesaver and can prevent you from ruining your credibility as a trustworthy business partner.

> "Become that rare person where people know that your word is your bond and you're going to do exactly what you say you're going to do."[96]
> —John W. Rogers Jr., investor

Pay for Proximity

Why: There is power in proximity. When you're just starting out, sometimes you must pay for it. Spending time around wealthy people will help you build confidence, show you what is possible, and give you the power to improve your financial situation. I am here to tell you that you should be prepared to pay to be in the proximity of these people. It can mean paying for coaching, paying for investment help, paying to attend masterminds, paying to attend in-person events, or paying to attend retreats. This one is sometimes hard to wrap your mind around. When was the last time you actually paid money to make money? The ROI is often unpredictable, which is why most people won't do it. The collective energy of a room full of wealthy individuals is hard to describe, but it feels amazing, and can pay dividends.

My Experience: The first event I paid to attend was Greg Reid's Prosperity Camp. Wow. There were only about 50 people in attendance, and as a participant, you could talk to anyone. I was literally rubbing elbows with millionaires, billionaires, and business celebrities. I couldn't believe events like these existed, and all I had to do was buy a ticket. I walked out of that event feeling like a million bucks with a pocketful of business cards and a phone full of selfies. Missing events like these and the opportunities they'll bring to increase your wealth has a huge opportunity cost.

Pro Tip: When you're attending events, make sure you can clearly answer the question, "What do you need help with?" I didn't expect to be asked this question so many times by people who genuinely wanted to help. Answering, "Uh, I don't know," is not acceptable. It's a wasted opportunity not to define what you need help with before attending these events. Then, when someone asks you, be honest and tell them what it is you're looking for. Worst case, they can't help you. Best case, they make your dreams come true.

> *"Courage starts with showing up and letting ourselves be seen."*[97]
> —Brené Brown, author of *Daring Greatly*

Host a Mastermind Group

Why: A mastermind group is a peer-to-peer mentoring group that helps members level up in life with feedback and advice from the other members. Masterminds can have specific themes or be open-ended. Leaders and innovators, like Benjamin Franklin, Thomas Edison, and Walt Disney, all participated in mastermind groups and used them to improve their thinking and move faster through life. Through sharing your ideas, you can increase the amount of feedback and suggestions you receive on big decisions, which improves your chances of success. Group members will also push you to think bigger and offer different perspectives on how to achieve your goals. Groups range in size from three to dozens of participants, but I recommend choosing a smaller group so that you can get more floor time and personalized feedback. These groups usually have rotating moderators and follow a strict group structure, allowing each member to present situations and receive feedback. By starting a mastermind group yourself, you can choose the frequency, duration and theme of the meetings, and have a say about who joins.

My Experience: I first read about the concept of masterminds in Napoleon Hill's *Think and Grow Rich*. My friend Alec and I started meeting regularly and our first business, BookThinkers, was born as a result. Thinking about it, everything I have in life is because of masterminds. You never know what can happen when you start trading ideas with other people on a regular basis, just like I talked about back in Chapter 8. If you're looking to start a mastermind, that would be a great chapter to revisit.

Pro Tip: You can make money from hosting mastermind groups by charging a monthly subscription or annual sum to participants. Useful books, like *The 8-Minute Mastermind* by Brad Hart, can assist you if you're interested in setting one up.

> "If you have an apple and I have an apple and we exchange these apples then you and I will still each have one apple. But if you have an idea and I have an idea and we exchange these ideas, then each of us will have two ideas."[98]
>
> —George Bernard Shaw, playwright

Improve Your Memory

Why: In Kevin Horsley's book, *Unlimited Memory*, he says, "Learning and memory are the two most magical properties of the human mind. Learning is the ability to acquire new information, and memory holds the new information in place over time. Memory is the foundation to all learning. If memory is not set in place, all you are doing is throwing information into a deep hole never to be used again. The problem is that many people are not recalling what they know, and they are constantly learning and forgetting, and learning and forgetting, and learning and forgetting…" Without a great memory system, you are limiting your ability to implement the amazing things you read and learn from books, classes, podcasts, seminars, or mentors. Continuing to learn without improving your memory has a major opportunity cost.

My Experience: "Sorry, what was your name again?" was a question I had to embarrassingly ask for far too long. After reading Kevin's book and watching his TED Talk, I completely changed my view of memory. I always thought I just had a bad memory. What I had was a bad set of memory systems. After implementing what I learned, I started retaining more information from daily interactions, such as names, as well as information from the books I was consuming. Now, I am confident in my memory, and I would say I have one of the best brains out there!

Pro Tip: Like anything else, practice creates progress. Kevin outlines some exercises you can practice regularly to actively improve your memory and be more confident in the supercomputer between your ears. Read his books!

> *"Memory is the cornerstone of our existence. It determines the quality of our decisions and, therefore, our entire life."*
> —Kevin Horsley, author of *Unlimited Memory*

Practice Extreme Ownership

Why: Extreme ownership is the practice of taking responsibility for everything in your life to an extreme degree. From a leadership perspective, it means you become responsible for your actions, as well as the actions of your team. Two Navy SEAL officers, Jocko Willink and Leif Babin, created this philosophy in their book, *Extreme Ownership*. As a leader, in your personal or professional life, you must start by realizing that there are no bad teams or families, only bad leaders. If another leader could step into your shoes with the same team and the same resources and do better, that means you have room to grow. Recognizing this and checking your ego at the door will start to motivate you to do better in life or at work. There is nothing worse than blaming others for the failures of your team or of yourself. Take ownership. Take extreme ownership.

My Experience: For some reason, in the workplace, most people tend to play the role of a victim when they first start. "My boss made me do this. I hate that I must do that." After reading *Extreme Ownership*, I completely changed my perspective on what it means to take ownership of your life. If you don't take responsibility, who will? Now, no matter my direct involvement in a situation, I am always the first person to take responsibility for the outcome and work to improve our chances of success for the next attempt. Blaming others is just not acceptable.

Pro Tip: One of my favorite lessons from the book was that even as an employee, you should take responsibility for your bosses. You should lead up the chain of command. Why? Because you can. That is what a leader does. They take as much responsibility as they can instead of making excuses. This attitude will help you grow faster.

> *"Leaders must own everything in their world. There is no one else to blame."*[100]
>
> —Jocko Willink, co-author of *Extreme Ownership*

Practice Idea Sex

Why: Idea sex is a process where two or more distinct ideas "mate" and produce new ideas as a result. Author James Altucher made the term popular. Many well-known authors and innovators use the practice to drive creativity. Simply take some random subjects and pair them to see the potential fun and unique results. This will force you to create new connections in your brain and, occasionally, something useful may result from them. Let's use a wealth example. Maybe your task is to "mate" the idea of investing your money with your favorite sport, football. As you start to pencil ideas, there will be some zany or unrealistic "idea children," such as buying your local football team (does anyone have a few billion lying around?) as well as practical "idea children," such as investing in a T-shirt printing press so that you can start making witty football shirts and selling them online. The point is to flex those creative muscles more often and increase the chances that you'll eventually have a novel idea that will dramatically improve your wealth.

My Experience: After reading James Altucher's book, *Choose Yourself!*, I was fascinated by the concept of idea sex. James used it to write entertaining articles, but I was interested in how to use it to create new ideas for my business and fresh content for my social media. How can I combine books with travel? Or maybe books with airplanes? Although most of the novel concepts I come up with are goofy, from time to time, there are some great outcomes and I get to have fun while bolstering my creativity.

Pro Tip: Simply pick two ideas related to your personal or professional life, set a three-minute timer, and come up with a minimum of 10 ideas. The first few ideas normally come easy, but the next couple will be difficult. Push through, have fun, and watch the magic happen. If you want to try this now and don't have any ideas, try combining 'wall art' and 'headphones' and see what you come up with.

> *"Business is just a vehicle for transforming the ideas in your head into something real, something tangible, that improves the lives of others. To create something unique and beautiful and valuable is very hard. It's very special to do. It doesn't happen fast."*[101]
> —James Altucher, author of *Choose Yourself!*

Practice Book Sex

Why: Let's say you're reading two unrelated books. The first is a biography of one of your favorite entrepreneurs and you're reading it because you want a better understanding of how to delegate tasks to your employees. The second is on the science of intermittent fasting, and you're reading it because a mentor mentioned to you that fasting has really boosted her energy recently and you've been feeling kind of lethargic. Since both books are fresh in your mind, you start merging the two ideas together...aka Book Sex. The result? You come up with a fun idea. You could also call these Book Babies. So now, instead of delegating tasks in real-time, you decide to restrict your delegation to specific times during the week. This way, you can group activities together and limit the number of times you disrupt your employees' workdays. Does intermittent delegation work? I don't know. But you never would have thought of it unless you were reading both books and open to merging them together. If you're taking great notes from the books you're reading, you can also do this intentionally by taking notes from different books and journaling about how they might work together.

My Experience: Many of the Healthy, Wealthy, and Happy Habits I outlined in the back of this book were the result of Book Sex sessions. Combining ideas from my favorite books allowed me to constantly innovate and reference older book notes, which consequently improved my life. Joining James's Idea Sex concept with personal development books was how I originally came up with this practice.

Pro Tip: Mate personal finance and investing books together for novel money ideas. For example, what might happen if you mated The *Psychology of Money* by Morgan Housel with *Profit First* by Mike Michalowicz? There is always room for innovation, and I believe this practice is one of the best ways to facilitate more of it.

> *"You will be the same person in five years as you are today except for the people you meet and the books you read."*[102]
> —Charlie "Tremendous" Jones, author of *Life is Tremendous*

Snowball Debt

Why: Do you have a lot of debt? If so, applying the following strategy to paying off your debt will make it less intimidating. Dave Ramsey coined the term "snowballing debt" in his book, *The Total Money Makeover*. It involves compiling a list of all your debt accounts from smallest to largest. In your list, make sure you note the total amount owed, the minimum amount due, and the due dates for each payment. Next, budget beyond the minimum you have to pay for each account. Once you have that amount, start applying it to your smallest debt account until it's wiped out. Next, take that budgeted amount and the minimum you were previously paying to the smallest account and apply both to the next one. As you continue this process, over time, you'll accumulate a debt snowball that gets larger and larger. This strategy, as opposed to paying your highest interest accounts first, leverages the psychological principle of momentum to destroy debt. Watching your first couple of debt accounts disappear is a wonderful feeling.

My Experience: Around the time I was graduating from college, I had quite a few different debt accounts, ranging from credit cards to car loans and student loans. Using Dave Ramsey's snowball technique, I was able to get organized and then systematically eliminate all my small debt accounts within the first 12 months after graduation. Over the following years, I became debt-free outside of my college loans. This technique seems like magic, but it truly works to get debt under control.

Pro Tip: Not all debt is created equal. Although for the right person, there are psychological benefits to paying down debt early, some debt accounts like college loans carry very low interest rates. Depending on the interest rates, you might be better off investing that money and just paying minimums. Plus, credit scores are boosted when you have a long payment history of on-time payments. Consult an expert, but I have found this investment vs. debt strategy to pay off in a big way.

> *"Winning at money is 80% behavior and 20% head knowledge. What to do isn't the problem; doing it is. Most of us know what to do, but we just don't do it. If I can control the guy in the mirror, I can be skinny and rich."*[103]
>
> —Dave Ramsey, author of *The Total Money Makeover*

Create a Wealth Accountability Group

Why: Have you heard of Tiger 21? It's an exclusive network of wealthy individuals, current and former entrepreneurs, investors, and executives who meet on a regular basis to review each other's financial portfolios. The group becomes your own personal board of financial advisors and directors. Group members take turns presenting their entire financial portfolio, with complete transparency. Imagine standing in front of a room and having to defend each investment decision and major expense. Daunting, right?

Well, that group is exclusive, but you can create your own version of it within your network. You'll need a few friends with growth mindsets who are willing to share their financial pictures, and then you can use the Success Buddies framework I described earlier in the book to set up and manage a recurring accountability group.

My Experience: Although I have not implemented this yet, I am in the process of putting together my first group. I originally heard about it on the *My First Million* podcast after my friend Marcus shared an episode where the two hosts interviewed Rob Dyrdek. Rob explained his experience with Tiger 21, and it sounded fascinating.

Pro Tip: The best time to start one of these groups was yesterday. Get on it. I imagine most people go their entire lives without having to open the books and defend their portfolio. I can only imagine that the benefits of doing this are extraordinary. Plus, since you're the average of the five people you spend the most time with, this is an excellent way to be around wealthier people.

> *"Accountability breeds responsibility."*[104]
> —Stephen R. Covey, author of *The 7 Habits of Highly Effective People*

Wealthy Friends

Why: If you spend more time with wealthy people, you'll become wealthier. The influence of the people you spend time with is not always obvious, but it is consistent. Instead of sitting around with your friends and gossiping about other people, you'll find yourself talking about the latest wealth trends, opportunities for investment, and productivity hacks. These small differences in conversation will compound, leading you to a wealthier lifestyle. If you can't find wealthy friends, make them. Introduce your existing network to books like this and talk with them about the benefits of implementing these wealthy habits. Help your friends see these habits through the positive and exciting lens that you do, and it will rub off on them.

My Experience: At college, I noticed many of the business students having conversations about money I didn't understand. So I decided to read some personal development books. Almost immediately, I was not only participating in those conversations, but leading them. Do you see how spending time around them helped to highlight my areas for improvement and passively encouraged me to close the gap? Now, I spend my time actively seeking people who have done what I want to do financially so that I can learn from them.

Pro Tip: Who do you spend the most time with? For me, it is my wife. That means, mathematically, outside of myself, she has the biggest impact on my wealth. Getting her involved in the wealthy habits mentioned throughout this chapter has helped me compound and reinforce the benefits of everything we do. Having money-related conversations with a significant other can be difficult, but it's worth it. Become a team and tackle these subjects together.

> *"It costs nothing to ask wise advice from a good friend."*[105]
> —George Clason, author of *The Richest Man in Babylon*

Wealthy Mentors

Why: Earlier in the book, we talked about a realization I had when I first began my personal development journey where I found that by reading a book, I was condensing decades of someone else's experience into mere days of self-education. Mentors don't have to meet with you in person. Sometimes, they mentor you through the books they've written. Hear me out: personal experience is a great teacher, but other people's experiences are sometimes better.

By studying wealthy people and learning about the wealthy habits they put in place, you will find new concepts to implement into your life. If you want to earn a million dollars, study the profiles of some successful multi-millionaires or billionaires. If you want to start a business, study some successful serial entrepreneurs who have started a handful of businesses. If you want to become a minimalist and cut most of your expenses, study a group of monks who have given up all worldly possessions and see how they are able to manage. By studying people who have done what you want to do and have done it well, you will realize what the human brain is capable of, and it will encourage you to push your wealth boundaries even further.

My Experience: As Robert Kiyosaki and Sharon Lechter teach us in *Rich Dad Poor Dad*, the subject of money is not taught in school; it is only taught and experienced at home. That means if you come from a low-income family, you're going to learn poor or middle-class money habits if you don't choose to break the cycle and adopt wealthy mentors. All the insights in this book came from studying the amazing men and women who have taken the time to teach me through their written word. I will continue studying and surrounding myself with wealthy people for the rest of my life.

Pro Tip: These wealthy mentors are easier to reach than you think. Through running a personal development podcast for the last few years, I have been able to interview some of my favorite wealthy mentors and use those conversations for personal mentoring. These authors are usually driven by a purpose to help their communities become wealthier. By asking them great questions, you'll often get great responses.

> *"Show me a successful individual and I'll show you someone who had real positive influences in his or her life. I don't care what you do for a living—if you do it well, I'm sure there was someone cheering you on or showing the way. A mentor."*[106]
>
> —Denzel Washington, actor

Follow Wealthy People

Why: In the same way that you become the average of the five people you spend the most time with, you also become the average of your social media feed. If your feed is full of 'un-wealthy' behavior, it will negatively impact your wealth. If your feed is full of wealthy and motivational behavior, it will positively impact your wealth. We are always consuming information, whether consciously or subconsciously, so make your feed overwhelmingly packed with wealth-focused information, especially if you're spending a good amount of time scrolling on social media. I love reading books, but I have also found some valuable information by following wealthy people on social media—it's a great platform for wealthy authors to provide updates on the content in their books or provide additional information their readers are looking for.

My Experience: I first became aware of the toxic wealth-related content on my Instagram feed after college. I was following a bunch of accounts that posted luxury cars and huge mansions but didn't teach me anything or provide real value. They encouraged me to desire these unrealistic assets and to party all the time. By consciously going through my feed and removing the bad accounts, I was heading in the right direction. After that, I started adding educational accounts and those of authors of books about wealth to my feed and eventually, the algorithm changed in my favor. These small but subtle changes in my life will compound and have much larger impacts over time.

Pro Tip: Survey your wealthiest friends and ask who they follow for wealth-related tips. You'll be surprised how many accounts exist that you'd never stumble onto, yourself.

> *"It is not much different from a person who goes to the gym to exercise on a regular basis versus someone who sits on the couch watching television. Proper physical exercise increases your chances of health, and proper mental exercise increases your chances for wealth. Laziness decreases both health and wealth."*[107]
> —Robert Kiyosaki, author of *Rich Dad Poor Dad*

Happy Habits

Practice Gratitude

Why: Gratitude involves expressing thanks or appreciation for something in your life. Gratitude can range from the feeling of joy you get from your favorite book to acknowledging the clean drinking water you have access to or the food on your dinner table. There are many ways to practice gratitude, including exercises like journaling, simply paying attention to the world around you, complimenting a friend or family member, a random act of kindness, meditation, or prayer. Regular gratitude has shown to have a very positive impact on your mental health. It can ease symptoms of anxiety and depression, boost your mood, improve your relationships, and increase optimism.

My Experience: I started practicing gratitude about six years ago. I wrote down three simple things I was grateful for in a notebook every morning before work. Then, I graduated to journaling in an Evernote document, sometimes writing a few paragraphs about each thing I was grateful for. It has had such a big impact on me that eventually, I got the numbers 1) 2) 3) tattooed on my left wrist so that each morning I could use that trigger to practice gratitude. Throughout the day, I would refocus my attention on the tattoo any time I felt ungrateful or resentful. Gratitude has changed my life.

Pro Tip: If tattoos are not your thing, you could write "What are you grateful for today?" on a sticky note and place it next to your bathroom mirror. Then each time you brush your teeth, focus on something you're grateful for and start to rewire your brain to concentrate on gratitude.

> *"It's not the happy people who are grateful; it's the grateful people who are happy."*[108]
>
> —Gaur Gopal Das, author of *Life's Amazing Secrets*

Meditate

Why: Meditation is the process of training your attention and awareness to achieve a mentally and emotionally calm and stable state of mind. The goal of meditation is not to turn off your mind, but to become more aware of your thoughts. You want to slow things down. There is no "right" way to meditate. I recommend simply sitting in a quiet place and setting a 10-minute timer on your phone. Close your eyes and do your best to focus on your breathing. It will be hard at first and you'll struggle, but over time, you'll start to experience the benefits.

My Experience: After reading *Tools of Titans* by Tim Ferriss, I was surprised to find that more than 80% of the world-class performers he interviewed for the book practiced some form of daily meditation or mindfulness. I didn't need any more convincing. I started meditating each morning before work, right after my gratitude practice. Using the Headspace app, I would sit down for 10 minutes and follow a guided meditation. The biggest benefit for me was increased emotional intelligence. It felt as though I was being given more time between an input to my brain and my reaction to it. I matured emotionally. I maintain a daily meditation practice to this day.

Pro Tip: For the more serious meditation nerds out there, I recommend trying the Muse brain-sensing headband. This device provides real-time feedback on your brain activity, heart rate, breathing, and body movements while you're meditating to help you improve your practice. The experience of getting real-time commentary on your brain activity is fascinating—I have used this product in over 100 sessions to date.

> *"All of humanity's problems stem from man's inability to sit quietly in a room alone."*[109]
>
> —Blaise Pascal, *Pensées*

Journal

Why: Journaling is the process of writing down your thoughts and feelings to understand them more clearly. If you struggle with stress, depression, or anxiety, keeping a journal can help you gain control of your emotions and improve your mental health. There is no "right" way to journal. The goal is just to start thinking and writing, writing and thinking. Your journaling can be written down on paper, typed onto a computer screen, or spoken into your phone. I recommend doing some research online and finding a set of writing prompts you're interested in to focus your thoughts. There are writing prompts on almost any topic, including health, wealth, and happiness.

My Experience: My first journaling was related to gratitude. Each day, I would write down three things I was grateful for and expand on why. Then, I turned to *The Daily Stoic Journal* by Ryan Holiday as I started studying Stoicism. I kept that journal going for years and really enjoyed the writing prompts. More recently, I adopted a process from Julia Cameron's book, *The Artist's Way,* called "morning pages," which consist of writing three long-hand pages right when you wake up. They can be about anything. I enjoy this practice because it warms me up for other types of writing, just like an athlete stretches before they work out.

Pro Tip: Keep your journals! From time to time, I flip back through my old gratitude journals, daily Stoic journals, and morning pages. Not only are they interesting to read, but as you work to improve your happiness, you'll be able to see how far you've come.

> *"I don't journal to 'be productive.' I don't do it to find great ideas or to put down prose I can later publish. The pages aren't intended for anyone but me. It's the most cost-effective therapy I've ever found."*[10]
> —Tim Ferriss, author of *The 4-Hour Workweek*

Use Affirmations

Why: Affirmations are positive statements that can help you overcome negative thoughts. Unfortunately, sometimes, people equate affirmations with wishful thinking and picture someone chanting, "I am rich!" in front of their bathroom mirror, hoping to magically find a million dollars in their bank account. That stereotype has pushed many people who would have benefited from daily affirmations away. Think of affirmations like this. Repeatedly going to the gym and working out will improve your physical health, right? We all know that. Well, repeatedly going into a positive headspace and repeating positive affirmations will help to reprogram your thinking. Over time, you will begin to think, and ultimately act, more positively. Earlier in the book, we discussed the reticular activating system (RAS), a network of neurons located in the brainstem that helps us to filter the countless inputs to our brain and to focus our attention on what matters. If you're always filtering for the negative, the unhealthy, and the poor, you'll find those things. If you start to filter for the positive, the healthy, and the wealthy, you'll find those things. Oftentimes, repeating affirmations, such as "I am healthy, wealthy, and happy" will lead to more real-life opportunities to become healthier, wealthier, and happier. Those opportunities didn't magically appear. They were always there. But now, you're filtering for them and seeing them clearly for the first time.

My Experience: After reading about affirmations in *Think and Grow Rich* by Napoleon Hill and in *The Miracle Morning* by Hal Elrod, I started printing out sheets of affirmations for the different areas of my life and repeating them many times per day. I loved it, and over time, I feel as though I have completely reprogrammed my brain.

Pro Tip: Use action-oriented affirmations, such as, "I am committed to achieving _____. There is no other option." Then, spice it up by adding intention. "I am committed to achieving _____ because _____." This is a powerful recipe.

> *"Attitude is a choice. Happiness is a choice. Optimism is a choice. Kindness is a choice. Giving is a choice. Respect is a choice. Whatever choice you make makes you. Choose wisely."[111]*
> —Roy T. Bennett, author of The Light in the Heart

Practice Visualization

Why: Visualization, in this context, is the practice of positive mental rehearsal. In the same way that affirmations can reprogram your subconscious mind so that it defaults to more positive thinking, visualization can improve your chances of success at a specific task. Think of an athlete running through plays in their head and watching themselves succeed in tomorrow's game, or a public speaker imagining themselves on stage and delivering their keynote. In both scenarios, they're using the power of positive visualization to improve their performance. If you're skeptical about visualization, think of how anxious some people are to fly in a plane. They have terrible mental images of what could go wrong, and that directly impacts their physiology. If you can create false realities in your brain that alter your physical reality, they might as well be positive, right? By spending time walking through an activity and visualizing your ideal outcome, you can generate positive emotions that will reduce stress, ease anxiety, build confidence, and increase happiness. After you have finished your affirmations (see the previous healthy habit), spend a few minutes walking through your most important meeting or task for the day. Ask yourself, "What does the ideal outcome look like?" or "How will succeeding make me feel?"

My Experience: As a big fan of the National Football League and their athletes, it was easy to adopt this practice after I read about so many of my favorite players using visualization to succeed. Now, I look forward to the way I feel when I visualize myself succeeding.

Pro Tip: Have you considered making a vision board? You know what I'm talking about...a poster board with all your dreams printed out and taped onto it. Although it sounds cheesy, I have been making one every year and find the experience very fulfilling. When I sit down to do my visualizations, I often use my board for inspiration.

> *"Everything is created twice, first in the mind and then in reality."*[112]
> —Robin Sharma, author of *The Monk Who Sold His Ferrari*

Define Your Ideal Day

Why: The Ideal Day Exercise is a visualization and journaling exercise used to create more clarity around what truly fulfills you. Instead of trying to define your entire future, which can be a large task and quite intimidating, we are going to take a more manageable approach here and work on identifying your ideal day. Without defining it clearly, how will you know when you have achieved it?

Grab a pen/pencil and a notebook, then sit somewhere quiet, close your eyes, and start visualizing. Imagine you're five years into the future, living your dream life, and planning out tomorrow's agenda. Be as detailed as possible and write out everything you can from the time you wake up until the time you go to sleep. Some questions to get you started: What time do you wake up? Where do you wake up? What's the weather like? Do you have a morning routine? What does that look like? What type of activities do you do throughout the day and why? What do you eat and drink? Do you exercise? Who else is involved in your day? By repeating this exercise annually, you can consistently work to close the gap between where you are today and where you want to be.

My Experience: I first heard of this concept from a podcast guest of mine, Jairek Robbins. After he described the activity to me, I thought I was in for an easy and lighthearted ten minutes. I was wrong. Instead of taking ten minutes to define your ideal day, it may take a few hours. Jairek recommended going as deep as you can, detailing every activity, emotion, and miscellaneous detail. I now complete this activity at least once per year so that I am always aligned with my ideal day.

Pro Tip: An important part of this exercise is to make sure the day you visualize is realistic and sustainable. Don't be tempted to simply fly through it by journaling that your ideal day is a beach vacation where you sip on margaritas until you pass out. That would be great for a few days, until you're sick and tired of it. The purpose of this exercise is to define a fulfilling life.

> *"The goal of the Ideal Day exercise is to illuminate the gaps between where you are today and where you want to be."*[113]
> —Jairek Robbins, author of *Live It!*

Make Fast Friends

Why: A fast friend is a stranger you meet while performing an act of kindness. I first learned about this concept during an interview with author Adrienne Bankert. She told me she always goes out of her way to demonstrate kindness, even to people she doesn't know. Whether she holds a door for someone in a rush, compliments a stranger's outfit, or pays for the person's coffee behind her in line, her goal is to make people feel seen and loved. She calls these people fast friends. These random acts of kindness can sometimes turn into long conversations, resulting in new friendships and meaningful moments in your life. Kindness is contagious, which means that the positive momentum you put out into the world can build its own momentum, impacting people far behind your initial interaction.

My Experience: I am so happy Adrienne introduced me to the concept of fast friends. These interactions feel small and sometimes meaningless, but that's okay. It's not about you. It's about helping other people feel special. The more often you attempt to make a fast friend, the more likely you are to positively impact someone who really needs it. Although it's not about you, it feels great to be of service to other people.

Pro Tip: I have read stories about people who were in such dark places, having had little to no positive interactions with, or acknowledgement from others for years. Then, out of nowhere, a stranger smiles at them, waves, asks them how their day's going, or performs some other small act of kindness. They become fast friends, and the trajectory of their life changes. It's as if momentum starts to shift in the other direction for the first time in a long time. Never assume you know what someone is or is not going through—just be kind to them. Imagine if everyone on this planet had that kind of mindset.

"Generous gestures spread just like gossip."[14]
—Adrienne Bankert, author of *Your Hidden Superpower*

Connect and Socialize

Why: Since 1938, Harvard has hosted one of the world's longest and most comprehensive studies on human happiness and well-being. Throughout this study, researchers have been following groups of people and comparing their happiness to several variables, including IQ, social class, income, genetic predispositions, and more. One of their biggest findings is that personal connection creates the most mental and emotional stimulation, which are automatic mood-boosters. On the other hand, isolation is a mental and emotional mood-buster.[115] These other variables we correlate with happiness, such as IQ or income, seem to have little or no association with happiness. The moral of the story here is that by deliberately working to connect with people and socialize, you're increasing your likelihood of happiness. These meaningful relationships will create more fulfillment for you than any of the other variables. Human beings are pack animals and are not meant to take on this world alone. When things go wrong in life, a solid support system and community to lean on will make a world of difference.

My Experience: I was blessed to grow up with such an amazing family and group of friends. Since I decided to work in sales and then social media, my network has continued to expand. I will never take that for granted.

Pro Tip: Schedule reminders to touch base with your friends. Although this sounds a little robotic, you don't want to let your most important relationships slip away. In this fast-paced world, it's easy to keep pushing back a reconnect call until, in the blink of an eye, years have passed. You owe it to yourself, now that you know the science, to go through your contact list and set up reminders to touch base with people who matter to you. For some relationships, that might mean weekly calls. For others, it might mean a call or meet-up every three to six months. The same goes with birthdays. Upload all your family and friends' birthdays to your phone and set reminders. That way, you'll never seem insensitive by forgetting to at least acknowledge people with a quick text. It feels good to be acknowledged.

> *"Happiness is the state when nothing is missing. When nothing is missing, your mind shuts down and stops running into the past or future to regret something or to plan something."*[116]
> —Naval Ravikant, entrepreneur and investor

Create a Happiness Mirror

Why: In *Can't Hurt Me* by David Goggins, I was introduced to the concept of an accountability mirror. The idea is that because you're in front of your bathroom mirror at least twice per day, you can use that space to create some accountability in your life. Here, we are going to modify David's idea and create a happiness mirror. Grab a bunch of sticky notes and write some uplifting messages on them. These messages should be overwhelmingly positive, just like your affirmations. Then, stick them on or next to your mirror. While you brush your teeth in the morning or wash your hands, read through your messages and internalize them. Then, do the same thing at night. If you work from home, even better, because you'll be in and out of the bathroom many more times. As you grow, read more books, and introduce yourself to more happiness-related concepts, you can update your sticky notes. I recommend doing this monthly so that you always have fresh awareness when you're reading them. By reading at least three positive sticky notes, twice per day, you'll end up reading over 2,000 messages per year. That's an amazing number. Every message counts.

My Experience: Positive triggers, like these sticky notes, have changed my life. I try to place positive environmental triggers all over my workspace. While writing this section, I realize that it has been a couple of years since I've deliberately followed through on this one. Time for some new sticky notes!

Pro Tip: If you work in an office, I recommend you create some happiness mirrors in your workplace. Tell your colleagues about the importance of subconsciously repeating positive messages and what type of impact it could have on their lives. Then, you can pass around sticky notes and encourage them to write a few and put them up. Now, not only can you take in your own positive messages, but you can also absorb the positive messages of others. A happy team is a better team.

> *"The most important conversations you'll ever have are the ones you'll have with yourself."*[117]
>
> —David Goggins, author of *Can't Hurt Me*

Define Your Purpose

Why: One of my biggest pieces of advice for young professionals is to define their purpose. The term "purpose" has become quite the buzzword and is sometimes difficult to define. I like to think of it as the action that creates the most fulfillment. In Evan Carmichael's book *Built to Serve*, you're guided through several exercises that help you articulate your purpose. As I followed Evan's process, I started to realize for the first time that I am motivated by progress. When I make progress in my health, wealth, or happiness, or when I help other people make progress in their health, wealth, or happiness, I am fulfilled. Evan helped me understand that my purpose comes from my pain. When I transformed myself from insecure and full of ego to secure and service-oriented, I became so much happier. That inflection point is important for me because, as I help other people go through that transition, I continue to feel amazing.

My Experience: Looking back, my purpose seemed to have been so obvious, but I could tell you that at the time, that was a breakthrough. I had read other books on purpose in the past, but none of them were as actionable as Evan's. Since then, I read some additional books on the subject I would highly recommend, such as *Black Sheep* by Brant Menswar.

Pro Tip: When you can clearly articulate your purpose, you become easier to follow on social media. For example, the moment I could communicate my purpose to my audience on social media, my following started growing much more quickly. When you are certain, you can provide more value, and an audience can certainly feel that. You become easier to work with too because other people now understand what motivates you. Purpose recognizes purpose.

> *"Your purpose is your source of power."*[118]
> —Evan Carmichael, author of *Built to Serve*

Create Memory Dividends

Why: Just like investors are paid dividends from certain types of investments, you can be paid memory dividends from certain types of life experience investments. I was first introduced to this concept in the book *Die With Zero* by Bill Perkins. For example, Bill explains that while you're traveling with friends, something hilarious might happen. Not only do you get a positive hit of endorphins from the original experience, but as you relive it over dinner a year later, you'll experience another positive hit of endorphins. How great is that? Something positive can be lived and experienced as many times as you like. I never thought of it that way. These investments in experiential memories can also compound, just like typical investments. Using the example above, let's say that as you retell the story years after it happened, someone at the table laughs so hard that they knock their glass of wine off the table. Now, as you retell the original experience, you can add the additional story of the toppled wine glass to make it even better. By documenting these experiences on video, as you age, you can maintain the memories and go back through an 'experiential highlight reel.' In the book, Bill talks about his aging father and how meaningful it was for his father to go through some old footage Bill dug up.

My Experience: I live for this! As I travel with family and friends, I make a big effort to document as much as I can so that we can relive these experiences with clarity. It will be fun to show my kids and grandkids these memories in the future and watch them compound and pay new dividends.

Pro Tip: Embrace discomfort. Some of my favorite memories to look through are the experiences that created the most initial discomfort. Videos from my international paragliding and skydiving excursions help to recreate the original adrenaline rush and leave me with a smile on my face. Now, I am always looking for the craziest and most unique experiences I can find.

> *"You retire on your memories. When you're too frail to do much of anything else, you can still look back on the life you've lived and the experience of immense pride, joy, and the bittersweet feeling of nostalgia."*[19]
>
> —Bill Perkins, author of *Die with Zero*

Embrace Discomfort

Why: Many people are limiting their potential because they are scared to embrace discomfort. I like to think of my comfort zone as a literal box, sitting in my house. Everything I can do without feeling uncomfortable sits inside that box. As I get outside my comfort zone, conquer the discomfort, and become comfortable with a new activity, I add it to my box. As this process continues, my comfort zone gets bigger and bigger. Since your potential is closely related to your ability to tolerate discomfort and try new things, the bigger the box gets, the more potential you have. Is this metaphor making sense? Using this logic, all your unfulfilled potential exists outside your comfort zone and it's your job to push those boundaries and add new items to the box whenever you can. Countless things in this world are sitting there, ready to bring you happiness you'll never experience if you continue to let discomfort deter you from experiencing them.

My Experience: When I first discovered that my potential sat outside my comfort zone, I started running full speed at useful skills that really scared me. A great example of this was public speaking and communication. Without constantly feeling nervous and sometimes sick to my stomach during door-to-door sales, phone sales, in-person sales, public speaking classes, and content creation, I would NOT be the person I am today. Was it painful? Yes. Was it worth it? Without a doubt.

Pro Tip: You don't have to eat an elephant in one bite. Instead of attacking your biggest fears in one fell swoop, work up to them through a series of small actions that compound and build momentum over time. For example, with my public speaking, I didn't try to land a TED Talk in week one. I started by having small door-to-door sales interactions thousands and thousands of times. This made my fears seem much more manageable.

> *"What we fear doing most is usually what we most need to do."*[120]
> —Tim Ferriss, author of *The 4-Hour Workweek*

Travel the World

Why: One of my favorite ways to create memory dividends and embrace discomfort at the same time is to travel internationally, especially to a country where I don't speak the language. I was inspired to take my first international solo-travel trip by my friend Derek after he visited Thailand and because of the book *The 4-Hour Workweek* by Tim Ferriss. After some deliberation, I decided to go to Buenos Aires for five weeks, without knowing anyone in the country and without speaking Spanish. As I recall from my first 24 hours in Buenos Aires, which was only about 3% of my trip, I had at least a dozen uncomfortable experiences I look back on now with a happy feeling. Personal growth usually feels uncomfortable while it's happening, but it feels wonderful in hindsight. I encourage you to try new foods while traveling, go on fun excursions, and meet as many local people and other travelers as you can.

My Experience: Many of my happiest memories have come from my time on the road, working from a coffee shop that barely had Wi-Fi ,while drinking some type of strange drink I couldn't quite understand when I ordered it. Travel offers a great perspective on your normal day-to-day life, highlighting what you don't look forward to going back to, and giving you a great opportunity to correct. Sometimes, you just need to step away from the hustle and bustle long enough to see that you're not as happy as you want to be. Plus, traveling opens your eyes to how the rest of the world lives. If you're like me and take for granted the freedom and economic opportunities a country like the United States offers, you'll be ever more grateful for them when you see what uphill battles other people are forced to face in certain parts of the world.

Pro Tip: Traveling internationally for long periods of time does not have to be expensive. If you're interested in learning more about how you can do this, I highly recommend reading the book *Vagabonding* by Rolf Potts. Rolf will show you that long-term world travel can be experienced for far less money than you're probably thinking, and he also shows you how to get the most out of your experiences.

> *"The value of your travels does not hinge on how many stamps you have in your passport when you get home—and the slow, nuanced experience of a single country is always better than the hurried, superficial experience of forty countries."*[21]
>
> —Rolf Potts, author of *Vagabonding*

Collect Happy Souvenirs

Why: A souvenir, or memento, is something you collect and keep in remembrance of a person, place, or event. It is usually put on display in your living space or workplace, and its meaning is unique to you. I was not a collector of souvenirs until I started traveling internationally. At many tourist destinations, locals set up gift shops where you can buy trinkets, such as pictures, statues, globes, postcards, clothing, or jewelry related to that location. At first, I purchased a couple of these items for friends and family members, but quickly, I found I was collecting them for myself. Once home, I realized that I could transport my headspace back to a happy memory simply by focusing on the souvenir. I used this trick whenever I was having a bad day, or when the weather was depressing. By going back in time to those happier moments, I could lift my mood and instantly feel better. This happiness habit is available to everyone, not just travel lovers. Start by thinking back to your happiest memories, and then display something related to that person, place, or event in your living space or workspace. Then, when you need to, use that item to go back in time and feel the positive emotions associated with it all over again.

My Experience: I have taken this habit to the extreme by getting tattooed when I travel to new countries. My travel tattoos are souvenirs, available to inject me with some happiness whenever I choose. For example, I have a tattoo of an hourglass on my left leg. The hourglass has sand up top, but as the sand falls, it forms an image of Machu Picchu, a site I visited with my wife. Those memories are some of my all-time favorites and my tattoo brings me a lot of joy when I look at it.

Pro Tip: Collect souvenirs of your greatest achievements, such as trophies or certificates. These will serve as visible reminders of how far you've come and what you've been able to accomplish. As the type of reader who has made it this far into the book, my guess is that you're success-oriented. If progress brings you happiness like it does for me, displaying these achievement souvenirs will ultimately bring you happiness and immortalize your happy memories.

> *"For as long as people have traveled to distant lands, they have brought home objects to certify the journey. More than mere merchandise, these travel souvenirs take on a personal and cultural meaning that goes beyond the object itself."*[122]
>
> —Rolf Potts, author of *Vagabonding*

What Irritates You?

Why: When was the last time something really irritated you? Was it someone cutting you off in traffic? Did you have a beach day planned and you woke up to rain? Did your significant other forget your anniversary—again? Spend some time and jot down a few of the first things that come to mind. In Don Miguel Ruiz Jr.'s book, *The Mastery of Self*, I learned that these disruptive events can be quite valuable. By taking the time to analyze each one and find its root cause, you can then dig it out by the roots so that it doesn't knock you off balance again. We don't like to feel angry, and losing control because of an external variable we can't directly control, like the weather, is silly once you think about it. Using weather as an example, you may not have realized you have no control over your irritation about it until you write it down. Does it make sense to relinquish control of your emotions over something as unpredictable as the weather? No. Of course not. The more you think about it, the goofier it seems. You may realize that by putting all your eggs in one basket—the day at the beach—you're leaving your emotional response up to chance. In this scenario, you could have an indoor backup plan next time you schedule a beach excursion so that your day isn't ruined if it rains.

My Experience: I had a very difficult time with this exercise at first. Analyzing your own brain and understanding how and why it works can be an embarrassing endeavor. Over time, though, I started having more positive responses to things that originally sent me into an irritated spiral. Less angry time. More happy time. Who doesn't want that?

Pro Tip: Keep a small journal with you so that you can briefly document each time something irritates you. This way, you can carry on with your day and give each experience the proper time it needs when you're home and in the right headspace. If you're not comfortable pulling out a notebook and are looking to be discrete, try using the notes app on your phone instead.

> *"Feel your emotions. Notice any negative emotions that come up for you while you are listening. For instance, do you experience fear? Anger? Sadness? What is the source of these emotions? If these emotions arise for you, finding their origin is where you will find your gift."*[123]
> —Don Miguel Ruiz Jr., author of *The Mastery of Self*

Forgive

Why: There are two types of forgiveness: internal and external. Internal forgiveness happens when you stop feeling angry or resentful toward yourself, whereas external forgiveness happens when you stop feeling angry or resentful toward someone else. Both are extremely important habits to engage in. In *The Four Agreements* by Don Miguel Ruiz, I learned that humans are the only animals on the planet that can pay for the same mistake more than once. We call it regret. You do something once in reality and then relive it in your head over and over, even when others have moved on. By starting to forgive yourself more, you can drop the weight you're carrying from mistakes you've made in the past. One common way to remove this emotional baggage is writing a letter to yourself where you detail what happened, why it happened, and how you've chosen to move forward in a better way. After you've written it down on paper, burn it and you'll feel the weight lift away. For external forgiveness, it's a bit simpler. First, create a list of those you currently resent. Then, pick up your phone and call the first person on the list. Let them know you're currently working through this book and an author is having you confront your pain. Tell them why you feel the way you do and that even if they don't feel they've done you wrong, it's important for you to verbalize the fact that you forgive them. Although simple, this step is incredibly difficult, awkward, and requires quite a bit of willpower. Once you've worked your way through the list, you'll feel like an entirely new person.

My Experience: I read about an external forgiveness exercise like the one I just mentioned in Vishen Lakhiani's book, *Code to the Extraordinary Mind*. I was feeling ready, so I dialed up some old friends and explained the situation. Each of them received the information well, and it felt like the resentment I had been holding on to instantly disappeared. What an incredibly happy feeling it left me with!

Pro Tip: Now that I understand how much resentment weighs on my emotional well-being, I forgive myself and others instantly. At the end of the day, we are all just human beings trying our best to navigate the world. Life is hard enough as it is. Don't make it harder on yourself by punishing yourself or others for simple mistakes.

> *"Unforgiveness is like drinking poison yourself and waiting for the other person to die."*[124]
>
> —Marianne Williamson, author of *A Return to Love*

Create a Virtual Time Capsule

Why: Traditional time capsules are physical containers that store objects chosen to be representative of the present time. They are then buried for discovery at some point in the future. Imagine digging up your old lunch box in the back yard and finding some of your childhood toys, photos, and a few other miscellaneous items. Wouldn't that be cool? Maybe you even buried one of these yourself when you were younger as a symbol of times past. The idea of a virtual time capsule is very similar. Every week, you can film a one-minute video recapping your week. Maybe you talk about someone you met, an event you attended, or a place you visited. Then, you upload your video to a cloud storage library and promise not to revisit it in the short-term. At the end of the year, combine all your videos and watch a 52-minute recap of your entire year. How amazing is that? You can use these videos to measure how far you've come, as well as see what made you the happiest during the previous year, so you can plan to do more of the same. This only takes one minute per week and then an hour or so at the end of the year. Think how great it will be for your kids or grandkids to watch these videos decades from now. Start today!

My Experience: In June of 2020, I pulled out my camera and filmed the first video. Although I have missed a few weeks, I now have well over 100 one-minute recaps and the number continues to grow.

Pro Tip: You may want to give your recaps a theme. For mine, I chose gratitude. Each week, I focused part of my recap on general items, such as milestones in my personal and professional life, and then on what I was most grateful for that week. Looking back at these videos makes me very happy and reminds me of how fortunate I am to live the life I live.

> *"The three big ones in life are wealth, health, and happiness. We pursue them in that order, but their importance is reverse."*[125]
> —Naval Ravikant, entrepreneur and investor

Quit Negative News

Why: Our minds are like fertile gardens. Whatever we choose to plant and nurture will grow and take on a life of its own. Visualize a real garden for a moment. If you want to create and maintain a beautiful and happy space, you will remove the rocks, pull out the weeds, raise beautiful plants, nurture those, and probably put a fence around your garden to keep intruders out. Then, if you want to harvest something, it's clean, organized, and easy to work through. On the other hand, if you neglect your garden, weeds will find their way in, and your fence may collapse. Your garden is now susceptible to attack and may fall apart as a result. Now, you're left with nothing but negativity. Unfortunately, so many of us allow negative news stories to act as weeds in our fertile gardens. Most major news networks make their money from advertising, which means they need to keep you on their channel for as long as possible. To accomplish this, news broadcasters produce exaggerated edits of reality, designed to pull you in and create division. If you're angry with what you're watching, you'll stick around. If you're very supportive of what you're watching, you'll stick around. Anything in the middle is boring and will cause you to leave. Celebrity histrionics and political drama do nothing to help you achieve your goals. These biased viewpoints and dramatized realities replace your positive plants with energy-sucking weeds. Even if you don't think you're being impacted by the negativity, remember, your subconscious is always on and consuming information.

My Experience: I have never been into the news, but I see a lot of people around me who go down that bridge every night and come back worse off. Burn the bridge. Quit the drama. Replace the negative news with positive personal development books and meaningful conversations.

Pro Tip: Ask yourself, "From where am I consuming the most negative information?" For most of us, the answer is either the news or social media. By quitting the news and removing negative social media accounts from your feed, you dramatically reduce your consumption of external negative data, thereby minimizing the overall number of your negative thoughts. Fight the positive fight!

> *"A man's mind may be likened to a garden, which may be intelligently cultivated or allowed to run wild; but whether cultivated or neglected, it must, and will, bring forth. If no useful seeds are put into it, then an abundance of useless weed seeds will fall therein, and will continue to produce their kind."*[126]
>
> —James Allen, author of *As a Man Thinketh*

Remove Inconveniences

Why: If something bothers you daily, it will bother you over 10,000 times over the next 30 years. Why tolerate that? In *Beyond Order*, Dr. Jordan B. Peterson talks about how minor inconveniences compound over time and eventually turn into major inconveniences. Imagine your significant other starts biting their nails every night at dinner. At first, you barely notice it and from time to time, you might point it out. You figure it's not worth fighting over, so you ignore it. Over time, though, your frustration starts to compound. Eventually, maybe a few years down the line, enough is enough and you burst out in anger. "STOP biting your nails!!! Enough is enough!!!" Your significant other, unaware of how this bothered you, is hurt by the lack of communication and the sudden unexplained outrage. To stop this from happening to you, I encourage you to deal with any minor inconveniences immediately. If the inconvenience is something you can solve by yourself such as a slightly unresponsive computer keyboard or a phone alarm you dislike, fix it now. If the inconvenience involves another person, vocalize it and explain what's bothering you. The short-term pain of confronting someone is often better than the long-term pain of tolerating an inconvenience and eventually letting it overflow into an angry outburst that the other person doesn't see coming.

My Experience: In life, sometimes we need to take two steps back before we can take five steps forward. Recently, I was bothered by how many emails I was typing up per day. So, I decided to spend a few hours creating some templates to replace most of the emails I was typing manually. The hours up front are now saving me multiple hours per week. Not only can I get more work done in less time, but I am also not frustrated by having to type up these emails manually anymore.

Pro Tip: This habit helps to keep your most important relationships as positive as they can be. It's funny how often a small inconvenience ends up compounding into something that ruins a friendship, a family relationship, or a romantic relationship. Please be conscious of these things and be willing to confront them. There is nothing more important than the health of these relationships and the happiness they bring us in the long run.

> *"We must all suffer from one of two pains: the pain of discipline or the pain of regret. The difference is discipline weighs ounces while regret weighs tons."*[127]
>
> —Jim Rohn, author of The Keys to Success

Embrace Radical Transparency

Why: Lying is an interesting subject because, for most people, the truth is not so black and white. Depending on who you talk to, there are different types of lies and they exist on a spectrum from harmless to harmful. Misleading other people requires you to manage multiple storylines, and that becomes increasingly complex as you continue to lie. Imagine you're in a room full of people, and you're trying to balance the stories you've told each of them and how those stories may or may not align with each other. On top of that, you have the truth—which only you know. What a bunch of unnecessary complexity. Plus, the more you lie, the more risk you're assuming. One day, these stories will catch up with you and everything could implode. Instead, radical transparency calls for you to simplify things by sticking to one version of reality—the truth. The truth is sometimes painful, but in the long run, it's always the safest bet. I first came across the phrase "radical transparency" in Ray Dalio's book, *Principles*. Ray teaches us how to leverage the truth in business, explaining that your business's credibility is built over the long term and that a single lie can ruin years of hard work.

My Experience: It's hard not to lie. Little white lies, especially the ones you say to avoid hurting other people's feelings, are hard to avoid. Over time, though, as you constantly remind yourself that radical honesty is the better long-term play, you'll stop using them. Living one version of reality has kept me happier and it has also kept my friends and family happier. Everyone knows where they stand.

Pro Tip: Implementing radical honesty into your personal and professional relationships is important, but you don't need to tell people you're doing it. By starting a sentence with "To be honest…" or "If I'm being honest…," you're implying you're not normally an honest person. Be conscious of this. Once you're aware of it, you'll start hearing other people use phrases like that nonchalantly. Instead, if you must preface a statement, try saying, "This might be tough to hear, but…" so that you can still communicate your message while preparing the other person for a difficult conversation.

> *"Every time you confront something painful, you are at a potentially important juncture in your life—you have the opportunity to choose healthy and painful truth or unhealthy but comfortable delusion."[128]*
> —Ray Dalio, author of *Principles*

Go Complaint-Free

Why: What is the opposite of gratitude? For me, it's complaining. Gratitude comes from focusing on what you have in life. Complaining comes from focusing on what you don't have. Gratitude brings us to the present moment to appreciate what is in front of us whereas complaining brings us to a future moment where we want things to be different than they really are. In *A Complaint Free World*, Will Bowen defines complaining as talking about things you do not want rather than talking about things you do want. It's a complaint if you want the person or situation changed. Will encourages his readers to participate in a 21-day challenge where you wear a purple wristband and switch it to the other wrist if you find yourself complaining. The goal is to go 21 days without moving the band to the other wrist to become a certified complaint-free person. In this challenge, talking poorly, aka gossiping about other people, also qualifies as complaining. Our goal is to focus on the positive aspects of our reality so that we can become positive and happy people.

My Experience: After reading Will's book, I decided to buy some purple bracelets and try his challenge, even though I thought I was already complaint-free. Well, I was wrong. At first, I was surprised to find myself complaining 15 to 20 times per day. As I followed through with the challenge, I worked my way down to a few times per day and ultimately, a few times per week. I was never able to successfully complete a full 21 days, but I noticed a massive reduction in my complaints.

Pro Tip: Go ahead and purchase a purple wristband or bracelet. They are inexpensive, so buy a few extra in case they break, or if you want to hand some out to others. Purple sticks out and will prompt people to ask what you're doing with your band. By talking about your challenge, you can encourage others to participate. Since you are the average of the five people you spend the most time with, a big reduction in complaining across your entire top five will have big benefits for you as well. This challenge will be much harder than you initially think, but that's what makes it such a valuable experience.

> *"Misery not only loves company, it derives validation from it."*[129]
> —Will Bowen, author of *A Complaint Free World*

Cultivate Strong Patience

Why: When I was growing up and acting impatient, my mom always kindly reminded me that "patience is a virtue," meaning that the ability to wait for something without getting angry or upset is a valuable skill, especially for an adult. In fact, I dedicated all of Chapter 10 to the concept of delayed gratification, which requires a boatload of patience. Many of the best things in life are worth waiting for. The more valuable something is, the longer it takes to achieve it. Otherwise, we would all have six-pack abs, millions in the bank, and constantly radiate happiness. Achieving these things, though, requires patience. I have found that the best way to practice patience is to refocus your attention from impatience to gratitude. If you're in a long line waiting to get your morning coffee, instead of dwelling on your wait time and continuously checking your watch, simply reflect on how amazing your coffee is going to be and that you can even afford one in the first place. Instead of focusing on how long you've been waiting in bumper-to-bumper traffic, refocus your attention on the fact that you have a car and somewhere to be. Turn up the volume on your audiobook or music and spend time in the present moment.

My Experience: Thanks to my parents' guidance, I have been working to cultivate more patience since I was a kid. Although my current levels of patience didn't really kick in until my mid-20s, I am so happy to have found them. You won't find me trying to move too fast through life!

Pro Tip: The more patient you become, the more you'll notice when other people are impatient. When you're around impatient people, verbally highlighting their impatience, especially if they're in an emotionally unstable headspace, is unlikely to help them. Instead, simply mention how grateful you are for the circumstance you're in. For example, let's say you arrived on time for a dinner reservation, but the waitstaff notified you and your significant other that it will be another 30 minutes until you can be seated. As your significant other starts to react with impatience, step in and say how happy you are to be out with them. Talk about how the food will taste even better once you're a bit hungrier and ask for a menu so that you'll be ready to order once you're seated.

"Patience attracts happiness; it brings near that which is far."[130]
—Swahili proverb

Listen More Than You Speak

Why: Have you ever heard the expression "God gave us two ears but only one mouth for a reason"? Should we, perhaps, listen twice as much as we speak? I think so. By speaking less and listening more, you can progress much faster in your personal and professional life, as well as create more happiness. As Robert Greene states in his book, *The 48 Laws of Power*, "Always say less than necessary." Not only do you avoid saying anything foolish, but you also create the appearance of meaning and power in business settings by staying quiet. In personal relationships, who doesn't love a good listener? One of the best ways to upgrade your listening skills is to improve your questions. As Voltaire said, "Judge a man by his questions rather than his answers."[131] A good question is something that requires the recipient to elaborate on a subject they're interested in. When you're talking with a friend, family member, colleague, or even a stranger, instead of asking a yes or no question, try asking a who, what, when, where, why, or how question. That will get the other person talking and will show them you're interested in learning more about what they have to say.

My Experience: Through my late high school years and even through my college years, I thought that to be successful, you had to have everyone's attention. I was wrong. Over the last few years, it has been my mission to listen more than I speak. As a result, life seems to be working out much better.

Pro Tip: When a friend is venting to you, ask them, "Are you looking for advice or for me to just listen?" I often assumed that someone was looking for advice when they just needed to feel heard and let off steam. This question saved me from giving out a lot of useless advice and improved my ability to listen.

> *"When people talk, listen completely. Most people never listen."[132]*
> —Ernest Hemingway, novelist

Zoom Out (Astronaut)

Why: Have you ever looked at photos of Earth taken from space? If not, you should stop right now and search for one. They are amazing. The incredible part is that you can just cover up Earth with your thumb. Gone. Our amazing planet is just a small dot in an infinite sea of other planets and stars. If you remove Earth, nothing changes. Our planet is full of wonderful people, architecture, works of art, ideas, and emotion. Even if all that disappeared, almost nothing would change in the grand scheme of things. What does this show us? It shows us not to sweat the small stuff. Life is too short, and this planet is too small for us to allow the smallest of inconveniences to throw off our entire day. To be reading this, your grandparents had to meet each other...and their grandparents had to meet each other. Can you believe how wild that is? Take advantage of this opportunity you've been given to live a fruitful life and do something positive with it. Living with this type of mentality allows me to stay positive and in control of my emotions in situations that used to throw me off.

My Experience: I saw a social media post where the creator wrote about the Sumerian people who, at one point, comprised the largest civilization on Earth. Their society had leaders, important people, influencers, etc. Now, we barely remember them as a people, much less individuals who thought they mattered. Don't fool yourself here. Most of what ruins our happiness is meaningless. Take the positive side of that and live your life, allowing yourself to do what makes you happy.

Pro Tip: I recommend setting your phone or watch wallpaper to a picture of Earth. Any time something bothers you, look at your phone or watch and be reminded of how little power that "thing" bothering you really has. Ask yourself, "How much will today's bothersome circumstance matter in 10 years? How about 100 years? Or 1,000 years?"

"And those who were seen dancing were thought to be crazy by those who could not hear the music."[133]

—Friedrich Nietzsche, philosopher

Plant Positive Trees

Why: Recently, I was listening to an author discuss relative spending. He was saying that he makes 200 times more than the average person, which means that every time he spends money on something like a dinner or a vacation, it only impacts his financial portfolio about 1/200th of the way it would impact him if he was making average money. This was fascinating to me because for him, a $100 steak dinner was only costing him $0.50, relatively speaking. Why wouldn't you go to dinner every night if that was the case? Well, I started thinking about how we can apply this to another pillar of life—happiness. When you are leaning into your purpose and you've planted a bunch of positive trees, aka happy habits, normal 'expenses,' aka things that normally cause you to slip into a negative mindset, will cost you less than they normally would, relatively speaking. In short, the more positivity you 'earn,' the less a negative experience will 'cost' you overall. Positive trees come in many forms, such as happy family relationships, happy work relationships, happy friendships, happy romantic relationships, the impact you make through your professional work, the impact you make through your side hustle, your charitable work, and more. If one of them falls out of sync for a little while, you're diversified, so instead of your entire positive portfolio being impacted, the cost is much smaller.

My Experience: When I had very little going on in my life, it was easy for one small thing to ruin my day because I didn't have anything else to fall back on. Now, when something negative happens, I just refocus my attention onto one of the many positive trees I have planted, including all the habits listed in this book. Instead of swinging from one end of the emotional spectrum to the other, my emotional floor seems to have risen quite a bit. The things that used to throw my headspace off for weeks I now shrug off without a second thought.

Pro Tip: By starting today and allowing your actions to compound, you're going to reach your dreams a lot faster than if you allow yourself to start tomorrow. I have kept the quote below on the wallpaper of my phone for a long time and reviewed it whenever I'm feeling a lack of motivation. It works wonders.

> *"The best time to plant a tree was 20 years ago. The second best time is now."*[134]
>
> —Chinese proverb

234

Write an Impactful Book

Why: One of the most interesting things about writing a book is that you do the work once, and then it lives on forever. I like to call that "passive impact." While you, the author, have moved on and are focusing on something else, a reader out there is consuming your book and learning from you. You're like a virtual teacher. I was first introduced to this concept of leverage through the work of Naval Ravikant. After reading his work, I started thinking about the ways I could impact people while I was sleeping. If I recorded a book review or a social media tip and posted it online, people could literally learn from digital copies of me while I was sleeping. How cool is that? Well, books do the same thing. Please do not underestimate the impact you can have on another person. I believe every person on this planet has something of value to say and to teach others. By communicating some of the biggest life lessons we have learned, we can help other people navigate the problems they're facing.

My Experience: I underestimated the difficulty of writing this book. As I sit here writing this sentence, I am about a year into the project and struggling to get it finished. I have learned so much about myself that even if I didn't sell a single copy, I would say I am happier because of my writing. It has allowed me to articulate my innermost thoughts and feelings in a way previously inaccessible to me.

Pro Tip: You don't have to be famous or an authority on a specific subject to write a book and make a positive impact. Many best-selling books are written by inexperienced first-time authors just looking to make a positive dent in the universe. If your intention is to help people, just get out your computer or a notepad and start writing. Even if you only sell one book and impact one life, I would consider that project a success.

> *"There is no greater agony than bearing an untold story inside you."*[135]
> —Maya Angelou, poet and activist

Create a Happy Accountability Group

Why: In the last chapter, we talked about a financial accountability group called Tiger 21. In this group, wealthy individuals meet on a regular basis to review each other's financial portfolios. What I am recommending here is to apply the same framework to happiness. The purpose of the group is to review each other's happiness portfolios and to give feedback and make recommendations. For example, what would happen if you gifted this book to a few friends and each month, you had some open discussions about the happy habits contained in this chapter? You could try meditation one month and visualization the next. Or perhaps encourage everyone in the group to make a vision board and present it to the group, explaining why each picture was selected, printed out, and glued on. The next month, you could do a 30-day journaling challenge and try to go complaint-free. Do you see what I mean here? Sometimes we think of happiness as a guarded secret, something to be tucked away and not spoken of. I think we should talk openly about it. It's well known now that emotions are contagious. It pays to be surrounded by positive people!

My Experience: My existing accountability groups function in this way already. Much of our conversations are focused on happiness and fulfillment. I can't believe that just a few years ago, these subjects felt taboo. My purpose? What makes me happy on the inside? I never would have thought that a bunch of my friends and I would be sitting around going as deep as we possibly could on these subjects. Now, during our talks, it seems like anything handled with less depth is a red flag.

Pro Tip: The best time to start one of these groups was yesterday. Get on it. I imagine most people go their entire lives without having to open their brains and defend their happiness portfolio. The benefits of doing this are extraordinary.

> *"One person's mood can affect both the mood of others and an entire group's collaboration and decisions."*[136]
>
> —Vanessa Van Edwards, author of *Cues*

Remember You Will Die

Why: *Memento mori* is a Latin phrase that translates to "Remember you must die."[137] At first glance, this seems dark and chilling, but hear me out. Too many of us overestimate the amount of time we have left on this beautiful planet, and as a result, we procrastinate and constantly put our dreams off until tomorrow. We end up regretting the time we waste on poorly leveraged activities, leading us to be unhappy. Constantly reminding ourselves we have a limited amount of time to chase our dreams allows us to prioritize our time more efficiently and take less of it for granted, leading us to get involved in more fulfilling activities.

Don't fall prey to the idea that you are going to live forever. Seneca reminds us of this in his book, *On the Shortness of Life,* where he says, "It is not that we have so little time but that we lose so much. ... The life we receive is not short, but we make it so; we are not ill-provided but use what we have wastefully."[138] Start focusing on this and let the magic of mortality guide your actions.

My Experience: I mentioned this earlier in the book, but I have the phrase *Memento mori* tattooed on my chest, right above my heart. Whenever I am feeling lazy or unproductive, I simply look in the mirror and focus on the heart beating below the tattoo. It won't beat forever. We are mortal.

Pro Tip: A company called 4K Weeks creates posters reminding people of impending death. The posters have 4,000 little squares, each representing one week of a person's life: 4,000 weeks divided by 52 weeks is 76 years—roughly the amount of time we humans have on this planet. By filling in one square a week, we remind ourselves that we don't have an infinite amount of time, so we should get out there and live life to the fullest.

> *"Before we go, if we should leave nothing else, we should leave a seed of benevolence. It is the very least we can do, and sometimes, that is all it takes."*[139]
>
> —Philip Gabbard, author of *THISday* and *Thrivation*

Declutter

Why: In *The Life-Changing Magic of Tidying Up*, author Marie Kondo takes us through the process of simplifying, organizing, and storing our belongings. The goal is to make our living spaces and workspaces places of peace and clarity. Marie teaches her readers that tidying up is not about being a neat freak, but that it is a spiritual experience. When we detox our physical spaces by removing clutter, we are also detoxifying our minds and bodies. Decluttering comes down to examining your relationship with every single item in your home and workspace. What you'll find is that each relationship is different, and as a default, we assign some type of significance to each item and defend why we need to keep it. Marie recommends asking yourself, "Does this spark joy?" If the answer is no, it might be time to let it go. Decluttering can be complicated. One of the best ways to simplify it and build momentum is to start with more functional items, like clothing, old documents, and other miscellaneous items. This way, you can feel the positive energy associated with simplifying your space and realize you're not going to miss items that don't truly spark joy.

My Experience: When we were growing up, twice a year, like clockwork, my mom asked us to declutter our closets and place unwanted clothing in our family donation pile. This habit is something we still practice today.

Pro Tip: Decluttering can certainly bring happiness and peace of mind by itself, but those feelings are compounded when you donate your clutter to those in need. Value is relative, meaning something that holds no value to you could change someone else's life. If you're decluttering your closet, find a local homeless shelter and see what they can use. If you're decluttering your bookshelf, donate books to your local library and see if they can put them to good use. This will leave you feeling amazing!

> *"The objective of cleaning is not just to clean, but to feel happiness living within that environment."*[140]
> —Marie Kondo, author of *The Life-Changing Magic of Tidying Up*

Compliment Everyone

Why: One of my early sales mentors, Michael, taught me the importance of complimenting other people. Everywhere we went together, I watched him compliment person after person after person, leaving each one of them with a smile. When we traveled for work, he literally complimented the TSA security personnel, the gate attendants, the airplane staff, the rental car associates, and every restaurant employee with whom we interacted. It was infectious. Since positivity is contagious, those people often complimented him back, creating a positive loop. How do people feel after they interact with you? Do you leave them feeling better than they did before? Some simple but powerful compliments include:

- I love your smile!
- I love your hair! Where do you get it done?
- I love your outfit! Where did you get that [insert outfit type]?
- What an amazing name! (after being introduced to someone)
- Your energy is infectious! What do you do to have so much energy?
- I wish everyone I interacted with was as professional as you!

My Experience: I could improve at this one, but I try my best to be like Michael! Since complimenting other people costs nothing, I try to do it as often as possible. You never know when a compliment is going to change the trajectory of someone's day. Our team at BookThinkers has a Slack channel where we document the random compliments we dish out each week as a way to encourage each other to do more of it.

Pro Tip: In her groundbreaking book, *Cues: Master the Secret Language of Charismatic Communication*, Vanessa Van Edwards gives us the ultimate formula: **warmth + competence = charisma**. Make this formula the blueprint for improving every interaction you have. If you audit your behavior and sense a lack of warmth or competence in your communication style, don't worry. Most people have an imbalance in this regard. Reading and applying what you learn in Vanessa's book can help improve your charisma and ultimately, the impact you make on other people when you compliment them.

> *"Too often we underestimate the power of a touch, a smile, a kind word, a listening ear, an honest compliment, or the smallest act of caring, all of which have the potential to turn a life around."*[141]
> —Leo Buscaglia, author of *Living, Loving & Learning*

Happy Friends

Why: It bears repeating that you are the average of the five people you spend the most time with. Well, if you hang around more with upbeat folks, you'll become happier. The influence of those you associate with is not always obvious, but it is consistent. Instead of sitting around with your friends and gossiping about others, you'll find yourself talking about the latest happiness trends, opportunities for boosting happiness, and happiness hacks. These small differences in conversation will compound, leading you to a more blissful lifestyle. If you can't find cheerful friends, make some. Introduce your existing network to books like this and talk with them about the benefits of implementing happy habits. Help your friends see these through your positive and exciting lens, and it will rub off on them.

My Experience: When your friends are constantly complaining about their lives but are seemingly unwilling to do anything about it, it can be hard on you if you're trying to be positive and as happy as possible. I experienced some difficulty on this and, as a result, I had to change some relationships. One thing that seemed to work well for me was sending over a few books on happiness and recommending that my friends thumb through them when so inclined. You can do likewise. By emphasizing the massive impact certain books have had on you, you might be able to trigger some more positive behavior in your friends.

Pro Tip: With whom do you spend the most time? For me, it's my wife. That means, mathematically, outside of myself, she has the biggest impact on my happiness. Getting her involved in the happy habits mentioned throughout this chapter has helped me compound and reinforce the benefits of everything we do. Having conversations with a significant other about happiness if one of you is struggling with it can be difficult but is always worth it. Become a team and tackle these subjects together.

> "But you are the average of the five people you associate with most, so do not underestimate the effects of your pessimistic, unambitious, or disorganized friends. If someone isn't making you stronger, they're making you weaker."[42]
>
> —Tim Ferriss, author of *The 4-Hour Workweek*

Happy Mentors

Why: Earlier in the book, we talked about a realization I had early in my personal development journey where I found that by reading a book, I was condensing decades of someone else's experience into just days of self-education. Mentors don't have to meet with you in person. Sometimes, they mentor you through the books they've written. Hear me out: personal experience is a great teacher, but other people's experiences are sometimes better. By studying joyful people and learning about the happy habits they put in place, you will find new concepts to implement into your life. If you want to meditate for an hour, study someone who has been on a meditation retreat. By studying people who have done what you want to do and have done it well, you will realize what the human brain is capable of, and it will encourage you to push your happiness boundaries even further.

My Experience: I have read many books on happiness and well-being over the last few years and implemented many habits. Everything in this book came from studying the amazing men and women who have taken the time to teach me, through their written word. I will continue studying happy people for the rest of my life.

Pro Tip: These happy mentors are easier to reach than you think. After running a personal development podcast for the last few years, I have been able to interview some of my favorite happy mentors and use those conversations for personal mentoring. These authors are usually driven by a purpose—to help their communities become happier—and by asking them great questions, you'll often get great responses.

"A mentor is someone who allows you to see the hope inside yourself."[143]
—Oprah Winfrey

Follow Happy People

Why: In the same way that you become the average of the five people you spend the most time with, you also become the average of your social media feed. If it is full of negative or unhappy posts, it will negatively impact your happiness. Conversely, if it is full of happy and motivational posts, it will positively impact your happiness. Your subconscious is always consuming data, so you'll want to curate overwhelmingly happiness-focused information, especially if you're spending a good amount of time scrolling on social media. I love reading books, but I have also found some valuable information by following happy people. Social media is a great place for happy authors to provide updates on the content in their books or provide additional information their readers are looking for.

My Experience: I first became aware of the toxic mental health- and happiness-related content on my Instagram feed after college. I was following a bunch of accounts where people complained about their situations instead of taking control of their lives. By consciously going through my feed and removing the bad accounts, I knew I was heading in the right direction. After that, I started adding happy authors and educational accounts to my page and eventually, the algorithm changed in my favor. These small but subtle changes in my life will compound and have much larger effects over time.

Pro Tip: Survey your happiest friends and ask who they follow for happiness-related tips. You'll be surprised how many accounts exist that you'd never stumble upon, yourself.

> *"The happiness of your life depends upon the quality of your thoughts: therefore, guard accordingly, and take care that you entertain no notions unsuitable to virtue and reasonable nature."*[144]
> —Marcus Aurelius, Roman emperor and philosopher

Final Words

Thank you for joining me on this reading journey. It is my hope that the pages of this book have provided you with insight, entertainment, and perhaps even inspiration. Your dedication to finishing this book is a testament to your love of reading, and I applaud you for it. As you move forward on your literary adventures, I wish you all the best. May you discover new books that captivate your imagination and broaden your understanding of the world. Happy reading!

Remember...the right book at the right time can change your life!!!

Please STOP and review this book!

Please take a few moments and leave a thoughtful review of this book on the platform where you purchased it. Your words have the power to influence other readers and help me reach the right people. Thank you for your kindness and generosity.

Bibliography

"92% of the U.S. Population Has Vitamin Deficiency. Are You One of Them?" *The Biostation*. February 3, 2014. https://thebiostation. com/bioblog/do-you-have-vitamin-deficiency/.

"#648—Clear, James. "Atomic Habits: Simple Strategies for Building (and Breaking) Habits, Questions for Personal Mastery and Growth, Tactics for Writing and Launching a Mega-Bestseller, Finding Leverage, and More." *The Tim Ferriss Show*. Apple Podcasts. Accessed January 29, 2023. https://podcasts.apple.com/ us/podcast/648-james-clear-atomic-habits-simple-strategies-for/ id863897795?i=1000592431628.

"#1080—Goggins, David. *The Joe Rogan Experience*. Spotify. February 2018. Accessed January 29, 2023. https://open.spotify.com/ episode/70ssh8DCCOlwwOEAjLobW3.

"*#1474*—Patrick, Dr. Rhona. *The Joe Rogan Experience*. Spotify. May 2020. https://open.spotify.com/episode/5dPiWhRGxso8rcctfJ7fC6.

Ali, Hamza. "Why Your Work Chair Might Be Killing You." CNBC. Accessed January 26, 2023. https://www.usatoday.com/story/money /business/2014/08/24/cnbc-sitting-at-work-health/14413451/.

Allen, James. *As a Man Thinketh*. Scotts Valley: CreateSpace Independent Publishing Platform, 2014.

Altucher, James. *Choose Yourself!* Scotts Valley: CreateSpace Independent Publishing Platform, 2013.

Alves, Glynda. "Exercising in the Morning and Doing a Second Wind Workout Is Robin Sharma's Key to Happiness." *The Economic Times*. March 7, 2019. https://m.economictimes.com/magazines/panache/ exercising-in-the-morning-and-doing-a-second-wind-workout-is-robin-sharmas-key-to-happiness/articleshow/68296313.cms.

"Americans Spend 293 Hours Driving Each Year." *Automotive Fleet*. September 8, 2016. https://www.automotive-fleet.com/136735/ americans-spend-an-average-of-17-600-minutes-driving-annually.

Angelou, Maya. *I Know Why the Caged Bird Sings*. New York: Random House, 2010.

Asprey, Dave. *Fast This Way*. New York: Harper Wave, 2021.

— — —. "Nicotine as a Nootropic, and Ways to Get it Without Smoking." Dave Asprey's website. https://daveasprey.com/ is-nicotine-the-next-big-smart-drug/.

— — —. "Make Your Coffee Work Harder for You." Dangercoffee.com. https://dangercoffee.com/pages/what-is-danger-coffee.

Aurelius, Marcus. *Meditations*. London: Penguin Classics, 2006.

Banayan, Alex. *The Third Door*. Sydney: Currency, 2018.

Bankert, Adrienne. *Your Hidden Superpower*. New York: HarperCollins Leadership, 2020.

Bennett, Roy T. *The Light in the Heart.* Roy Bennett, 2020.

"Binaural Beats: Sleep, Therapy, and Meditation." *Healthline Media.*
November 5, 2021. Accessed January 24, 2023. https://www.
healthline.com/health/binaural-beats.

Bowen, Will. *A Complaint Free World.* New York: Harmony Books, 2013.

Bryant, Adam. "A Great Teammate Is a Great Listener." *NY Times.*
February 15, 2014. https://www.nytimes.com/2014/02/16/business/
a-great-teammate-is-a-great-listener.html.

Brown, Brené. *Daring Greatly.* New York: Penguin, 2015.

Burg, Bob and John David Mann. *The Go-Giver.* New York: Penguin,
2015.

Buscaglia, Leo. *Living, Loving & Learning.* New York: Ballantine Books,
1985.

Carmichael, Evan. *Built to Serve.* Houston: Savio Republic, 2021.

"Circadian Optics Pitch Brings Mr. Wonderful to Tears." *Shark Tank.*
YouTube video. October 6, 2019, https://www.youtube.com/
watch?v=xjdPonNzYU8.

Clason, George. *The Richest Man in Babylon.* Scotts Valley: CreateSpace
Independent Publishing Platform, 2015.

Clear, James. *Atomic Habits.* New York: Penguin, 2018.

"Connie Stevens Quotes." *BrainyQuote.* Accessed January 29, 2023.
https://www.brainyquote.com/quotes/connie_stevens_197013.

"Cornelius J. Quotes" (author of *The Credit Repair Book*). Goodreads. Accessed January 29, 2023. https://www.goodreads.com/author/quotes/13767119.Cornelius_J_.

Covey, Stephen. *The 7 Habits of Highly Effective People*. London: Simon & Schuster, 2013.

Dalio, Ray. *Principles*. London: Simon & Schuster, 2018.

Das, Gaur Gopal. *Life's Amazing Secrets*. Gurgaon: Penguin Ananda, 2018.

De Bono, Edward. *Six Thinking Hats*. London: Penguin, 2016.

Definition of 'memento mori.' *Merriam-Webster*. https://www.merriam-webster.com/dictionary/memento+mori.

Drucker, Peter. *Managing Oneself*. Boston: Harvard Business Press, 2008.

"Ebbinghaus's Forgetting Curve." MindTools. Accessed January 22, 2023. https://www.mindtools.com/a9wjrjw/ebbinghauss-forgetting-curve.

Elkin, Elizabeth. "Anthony Bourdain's 10 Most Inspirational Quotes." CNN. June 8, 2020. https://www.cnn.com/ampstories/us/anthony-bourdains-10-most-inspirational-quotes.

Elrod, Hal. *The Miracle Morning*. London: John Murray, 2012.

Eyal, Nir. *Indistractable*. New York: Bloomsbury Publishing, 2020.

Ferriss, Timothy. *The 4-Hour Workweek*, Expanded and Updated. New York: Harmony Books, 2009.

Flynn, Jack. "20 Vital Smartphone Usage Statistics [2023]: Facts, Data, and Trends on Mobile Use in the US." Zippia. October 20,

2022. Accessed January 29, 2023. https://www.zippia.com/advice/smartphone-usage-statistics/.

Gabbard, Philip. *Personal Communication*. 2022.

Gach, Michael Reed. *Acupressure's Potent Points*. New York: Bantam, 2011.

Gardener, Chris. "The 1% Principle." *Medium*. August 3, 2018. https://the3fs.medium.com/the-1-principle-998b33512100.

"George Bernard Shaw Quotes." *BrainyQuote*. Accessed January 29, 2023. https://www.brainyquote.com/quotes/george_bernard_shaw_109542.

Goggins, David. *Can't Hurt Me*. Austin, TX: Lioncrest Publishing, 2021.

Go Lean Six Sigma. "The Best Time to Plant a Tree Was 20 Years Ago. The Second Best Time Is Now." September 24, 2018. https://goleansixsigma.com/the-best-time-to-plant-a-tree-was-20-years-ago-the-second-best-time-is-now-chinese-proverb/.

Guillebeau, Chris. *The $100 Startup*. New York: Crown Business, 2012.

Gundry, Steven. *The Plant Paradox*. New York: HarperCollins, 2017.

Hemingway, Ernest. "Ernest Hemingway Quote.". Accessed January 29, 2023. https://quotefancy.com/quote/803281/Ernest-Hemingway-Listen-now-When-people-talk-listen-completely-Don-t-be-thinking-what-you.

Hof, Wim. *The Wim Hof Method*. London: Rider, 2022.

Horsley, Kevin. "Instantly Recalling Understanding." TEDxPretoria. *YouTube* video. December 2, 2013. https://www.youtube.com/watch?v=EQc7MKtTzv4.

Horsley, Kevin. *Unlimited Memory*. Indiana: TCK Publishing, 2016.

Housel, Morgan. *The Psychology of Money*. Petersfield, England: Harriman House Limited, 2020.

"How Many People Are Dehydrated?" *Quench Water*. November 9, 2022. https://quenchwater.com/blog/how-many-people-are-dehydrated/.

Jensen, Kelly. "Over 50% of Adults Have Not Finished a Book in the Last Year." *Book Riot*. June 21, 2022. https://bookriot.com/american-reading-habits-2022/.

Jones, Charlie. *Life Is Tremendous*. Carol Stream: Tyndale Momentum, 1981.

Jorgenson, Eric. *The Almanack of Naval Ravikant*. New Delhi, HarperCollins, 2021.

Joshua, Anthony. "Cardio Is a Nice Way to Start the..." *What Should I Read Next?* Accessed January 27, 2023. https://www.whatshouldireadnext.com/quotes/anthony-joshua-cardio-is-a-nice-way.

Kiyosaki, Robert. *Rich Dad Poor Dad*. Lulu Press, 2016.

Koch, Richard. *The 80/20 Principle*, Expanded and Updated. New York: Broadway Business, 1999.

Kondo, Marie. *The Life-Changing Magic of Tidying Up*. New York: Random House, 2014.

Kwik, Jim. *Limitless*. Carlsbad: Hay House, 2020.

Lagacé, Maxime. "How To Be Happy: The 6 Happiness Pillars You Must Know." *Wisdom Quotes*. October 31, 2022. https://wisdomquotes.com/how-to-be-happy/.

"Les Brown Quotes." *BrainyQuote*. Accessed January 29, 2023. https://www.brainyquote.com/quotes/les_brown_387329.

"Life Expectancy." CDC. *FastStats*. February 7, 2023. https://www.cdc.gov/nchs/fastats/life-expectancy.htm.

Marcus, Aubrey. *Own the Day, Own Your Life*. New York: Harper Thorsons, 2018.

"Maximizing Productivity, Physical & Mental Health With Daily Tools." *Huberman Lab*, Episode 28, July 2021. Spotify. Accessed January 24, 2023. https://open.spotify.com/episode/72ejCLl57bquFBfEAjZEXU.

McKeown, Greg. *Essentialism*. London: Virgin Books, 2021.

Merton, Robert K. "The Matthew Effect in Science." Science. January 5, 1968. http://www.garfield.library.upenn.edu/merton/matthew1.pdf.

Michalowicz, Mike. *Profit First*. New York: Portfolio (reissue edition), 2017.

Miller, Jim. *Budgeting Doesn't Have to Suck*. Ron Miller's World Publishing, 2020.

Murray, Kelly. "I Wear My Blue Blockers at Night." Kelly Murray Sleep Consulting. February 3, 2021. https://kellymurrayadultsleep.com/articles/i-wear-my-sunglasses-at-night.

Nestor, James. *Breath*. New York: Penguin, 2021.

Newsom, Rob. "How Blue Light Affects Sleep." Sleep Foundation. Updated March 17, 2023. https://www.sleepfoundation.org/bedroom-environment/blue-light

Nietzsche, Friedrich. *A Quote by Friedrich Nietzsche.* January 25, 2023. https://www.goodreads.com/quotes/7887-and-those-who-were-seen-dancing-were-thought-to-be.

Noyed, Daniel. "Weighted Blanket Research Methodology." Sleep Foundation. March 11, 2022. https://www.sleepfoundation.org/research-methodology/weighted-blanket.

Pascal, Blaise. *Pensées.* London: Penguin Classics, 1995.

Perkins, Bill. *Die with Zero.* Boston: Mariner Books (reprint edition), 2021.

Philips, Kate. "20 Inspirational Quotes About Patience." *Country Living* republished by *Yahoo Finance.* April 22, 2020. https://finance.yahoo.com/photos/20-inspiratoinalquotes-patience-204700533/.

Plath, Sylvia. *A Quote by Sylvia Plath.* December 28, 2022. https://www.goodreads.com/quotes/8094-there-must-be-quite-a-few-things-that-a-hot.

Potts, Rolf. *Vagabonding.* New York: Ballantine Books, 2002.

Proctor, Bob. *A Quote by Bob Proctor.* December 5, 2022. https://www.goodreads.com/quotes/4473069-a-mentor-is-someone-who-sees-more-talent-and-ability.

Questlove: "The Only Mofos in My Circle Are People That I Can Learn From." QuoteFancy. Accessed January 29, 2023. https://quotefancy.

com/quote/1375496/Questlove-The-only-mofos-in-my-circle-are-people-that-I-can-learn-from.

Ramsey, Dave. *The Total Money Makeover*. Nashville: Thomas Nelson, 2013.

Rice, Jerry. *Jerry Rice Quotes* (author of *Go Long!*). Accessed January 26, 2023. https://www.goodreads.com/author/quotes/41758.Jerry_Rice.

Robbins, Jairek. *Live It!* Grand Harbor Press, 2014.

Robbins, Tony. *Life Force*. New York: Simon & Schuster, 2022.

— — —. *MONEY Master the Game*. New York: Simon & Schuster, 2016.

Rohn, Jim. *A Quote by Jim Rohn*. January 15, 2023, https://www.goodreads.com/quotes/209560-we-must-all-suffer-from-one-of-two-pains-the.

Ruiz, Miguel. *The Mastery of Self*. San Antonio: Hierophant Publishing, 2017.

Salmansohn, Karen. *Happy Habits*. Berkeley: Ten Speed Press, 2020.

Schwartz, David. *The Magic of Thinking Big*. New York: Simon & Schuster, 2015.

Seneca. *On the Shortness of Life*. New York: Penguin, 2005.

Sethi, Ramit. *I Will Teach You To Be Rich*. New York: Workman Publishing Company, 2009.

Sharma, Robin. *The Monk Who Sold His Ferrari*. San Francisco: HarperCollins, 1999.

Shaw, George. *A Quote by George Bernard Shaw.* January 8, 2023. https://www.goodreads.com/quotes/23088-if-you-have-an-apple-and-i-have-an-apple.

Solan, Matthew. "The Secret to Happiness?" Harvard Health Publishing. October 5, 2017. https://www.health.harvard.edu/blog/the-secret-to-happiness-heres-some-advice-from-the-longest-running-study-on-happiness-2017100512543.

Stevenson, Shawn. *Sleep Smarter.* Emmaus, Pennsylvania: Rodale Books, 2016.

Stone, Kevin. *Play Forever.* Austin, Lioncrest Publishing, 2021.

"Understanding Acute and Chronic Inflammation." Harvard Health Publishing. April 1, 2020. https://www.health.harvard.edu/staying-healthy/understanding-acute-and-chronic-inflammation.

"What's the Best Temperature for Sleep?" Cleveland Clinic. November 16, 2021. https://health.clevelandclinic.org/what-is-the-ideal-sleeping-temperature-for-my-bedroom/.

"Who Is 'The Iceman' Wim Hof?" Wim Hof Method. https://www.wimhofmethod.com/iceman-wim-hof. Accessed January 29, 2023.

"Top 13 Nutrients to Supplement for Long-Term Brain Health and Memory." Neuro Reserve. April 14, 2022. https://neuroreserve.com/blogs/articles/top-13-nutrients-to-supplement-for-long-term-brain-health-and-memory.

Tracy, Brian. *Eat That Frog!* National Geographic Books, 2017.

Twitter. Dr. Rhonda Patrick. Accessed January 29, 2023. https://twitter. com/foundmyfitness/status/1430938112369197061?lang=en.

Twitter. Naval Ravikant. Accessed January 29, 2023. https://twitter.com/ NavalismHQ/status/1505914323188731910.

Vaden, Rory. *Take the Stairs*. New York: Penguin, 2012.

Van Edwards, Vanessa. *Cues*. London: Penguin Business, 2022.

VanBuren, Dr. Kimberly. "Start the Reset Program." Balancing Act. https://www.balancingactlms.com/start-the-reset.

Walker, Matthew. *Why We Sleep*. New York: Simon & Schuster, 2017.

Washington, Denzel. "The Mentors He'll Never Forget." *Guideposts*. January 1, 2007. https://guideposts.org/positive-living/ the-mentors-hell-never-forget/.

Weil, Andrew. "Integrative Mental Health: A New Model for Depression Relief." *HuffPost*. March 18, 2010. https://www.huffpost.com/entry/ integrative-mental-health_b_354332.

Winfrey, Oprah. *Who Mentored You*. Harvard T.H. Chan School of Public Health. January 22, 2015. https://www.hsph.harvard.edu/ wmy/celebrities/oprah-winfrey/.

"Why Sitting Too Much Is Bad for Your Health." *WebMD*. January 25, 2022. Accessed January 26, 2023. https://www.webmd.com/ fitness-exercise/ss/slideshow-sitting-health.

Williamson, Marianne. *A Return to Love*. New York: HarperCollins, 2009.

Willink, Jocko. *Extreme Ownership*. New York: St. Martin's Press, 2017.

Wim Hof Quotes. Millyuns. https://millyuns.com/quotes-hof/.

Wolfson, Alisa. "Warren Buffett Says This Is the 'Biggest Mistake' People Make With Their Money (and Psst: It Has to Do With Savings)." *MarketWatch*. August 13, 2022. https://www.marketwatch.com/picks/warren-buffett-says-this-is-the-biggest-mistake-people-make-with-their-money-and-psst-it-has-to-do-with-savings-01659574976.

Zauderer, Steven. "Memory Capacity of Human Brain: 29 Human Memory Statistics & Facts."

Cross River Therapy. November 24, 2022. https://www.crossrivertherapy.com/memory-capacity-of-human-brain.

Endnotes

1   Charlie Munger, "Charlie Munger Quote: 'Those Who Keep Learning Will Keep Rising in Life,'" Create Yours, Accessed March 16, 2023, https://quotefancy.com/quote/1561910/Charlie-Munger-Those-who-keep-learning-will-keep-rising-in-life.

2   Kelly Jensen, "Over 50% of Adults Have Not Finished a Book in the Last Year," Book Riot, June 21, 2022, https://bookriot.com/american-reading-habits-2022/.

3   CDC, FastStats, February 7, 2023, https://www.cdc.gov/nchs/fastats/life-expectancy.htm.

4   Timothy Ferriss, The 4-Hour Workweek, Expanded and Updated, (New York: Harmony Books, 2009).

5   "Neuro-Linguistic Programming (NLP)," GoodTherapy®, September 15, 2009, https://www.goodtherapy.org/learn-about-therapy/types/neuro-linguistic-programming.

6   Merriam-Webster Dictionary, s.v. "memento mori," https://www.merriam-webster.com/dictionary/memento+mori.

7   Kevin Horsley, "Instantly Recalling Understanding," TEDx Pretoria, 2013, YouTube, December 2. https://www.youtube.com/watch?v=EQc7MKtTzv4.

8   Cross River Therapy, https://www.crossrivertherapy.com/memory-capacity-of-human-brain.

9   "Ebbinghaus's Forgetting Curve," MindTools, Accessed January 22, 2023, https://www.mindtools.com/a9wjrjw/ebbinghauss-forgetting-curve.

10 Jocko Willink, Extreme Ownership, (New York: St. Martin's Press, 2017).

11 Chris Gardener, "The 1% Principle," Medium, January 10, 2022, https://the3fs.medium.com/the-1-principle-998b33512100.

12 The Butterfly Effect, https://thedecisionlab.com/reference-guide/economics/the-butterfly-effect.

13 Merriam-Webster Dictionary, s.v. "ripple effect," https://www.merriam-webster.com/dictionary/ripple+effect.

14 Robert K. Merton, "The Matthew Effect in Science," Science, January 5, 1968, http://www.garfield.library.upenn.edu/merton/matthew1.pdf.

15 Matthew 25:29, Bible Gateway—new international version, accessed March 16, 2023, https://www.biblegateway.com/passage/?search=Matthew%2025%3A29&version=NIV.

16 "Spicy Nacho Tortilla Chips 16 Oz. Bag," Eat This Much, https://www.eatthismuch.com/food/nutrition/spicy-nacho-tortilla-chips-16-oz-bag,531301/.

17 Jerry Rice Quotes (author of Go Long!), https://www.goodreads.com/author/quotes/41758.Jerry_Rice.

18 "Top 13 Nutrients to Supplement for Long-Term Brain Health and Memory," Neuro Reserve, April 14, 2022, https://neuroreserve.com/blogs/articles/top-13-nutrients-to-supplement-for-long-term-brain-health-and-memory.

19 "Understanding the Pareto Principle," https://asana.com/resources/pareto-principle-80-20-rule.

20 Explanation of "amor fati," Mind Owl, https://mindowl.org/the-stoic-power-of-amor-fati/.

21 Seneca, On the Shortness of Life.

22 "How Many People Are Dehydrated?" Quench Water, November 9, 2022, https://quenchwater.com/blog/how-many-people-are-dehydrated/.

23 Kevin Stone, Play Forever, (Austin: Lioncrest Publishing, 2021).

24 "Maximizing Productivity, Physical & Mental Health with Daily Tools," Huberman Lab, Episode 28, Spotify, https://open.spotify.com/episode/72ejCLl57bquFBfEAjZEXU.

25 "Circadian Optics Pitch Brings Mr. Wonderful to Tears," Shark Tank, YouTube, October 6, 2019, https://www.youtube.com/watch?v=xjdPonNzYU8.

26 Andrew Weil, Founder and Director of The Arizona Center, "Integrative Mental Health: A New Model For Depression Relief," HuffPost, March 18, 2010, https://www.huffpost.com/entry/integrative-mental-health_b_354332.

27 Aubrey Marcus, Own the Day, Own Your Life, (New York: Harper Thorsons, 2018).

28 Dave Asprey, What Is Danger Coffee, https://dangercoffee.com/pages/what-is-danger-coffee.

29 Dave Asprey, "Nicotine as a Nootropic, and Ways to Get It Without Smoking," https://daveasprey.com/is-nicotine-the-next-big-smart-drug/.

ENDNOTES

30   Matthew Walker, Why We Sleep, (New York: Simon and Schuster, 2017).

31   Dave Asprey, Fast This Way, (New York: HarperWave, 2021).

32   Dave Asprey, Fast This Way.

33   Glynda Alves, "Exercising in the Morning and Doing a Second Wind Workout Is Robin Sharma's Key to Happiness," The Economic Times, March 7, 2019, https://m.economictimes.com/magazines/panache/ exercising-in-the-morning-and-doing-a-second-wind-workout-is-robin-sharmas-key-to-happiness/articleshow/68296313.cms.

34   The Biostation, https://thebiostation.com/bioblog/do-you-have-vitamin -deficiency/.

35   Steven Gundry, The Plant Paradox, (New York: HarperCollins, 2017).

36   https://millyuns.com/quotes-hof/.

37   "Why Sitting Too Much Is Bad for Your Health," WebMD, January 25, 2022, https://www.webmd.com/fitness-exercise/ss/slideshow-sitting-health#:~: text=Dementia%20Is%20More%20Likely&text=Sitting%20also%20 raises%20your%20risk,of%20all%20these%20health%20problems.

38   Hamza Ali, "Why Your Work Chair Might Be Killing You," CNBC, https:// www.usatoday.com/story/money/business/2014/08/24/cnbc-sitting-at-work -health/14413451/.

39   Amberlee Lovell Peterson, "Surprising Benefits of Chewing Gum," Select Health, https://selecthealth.org/blog/2017/04/surprising-benefits-of -chewing-gum.

40   "#1474—Dr. Rhona Patrick," The Joe Rogan Experience, May 2020, Spotify, https://open.spotify.com/episode/5dPiWhRGxso8rcctfJ7fC6

41   "Understanding Acute and Chronic Inflammation," Harvard Health Publishing, April 1, 2020, https://www.health.harvard.edu/staying-healthy/ understanding-acute-and-chronic-inflammation#:~:text=Research%20has% 20shown%20that%20chronic,to%20know%20its%20exact%20impact.

42   Karen Salmansohn, Happy Habits, (Berkeley: Ten Speed Press, 2020).

43   Anthony Joshua, https://www.facebook.com/themaclifehealth/photos/a.291 349081364014/502503013581952/?type=3.

44   James Nestor, Breath, (New York: Penguin, 2020).

45   James Nestor, Breath.

46   "The History of the Iceman Wim Hof," Wim Hof Method, accessed January 29, 2023, https://www.wimhofmethod.com/iceman-wim-hof.

47   "Who Is 'The Iceman' Wim Hof?" The Wim Hof Method, https://www. wimhofmethod.com/iceman-wim-hof.

48   "#1080—David Goggins," The Joe Rogan Experience, February 2018, Spotify, https://open.spotify.com/episode/70ssh8DCCOlwwOEAjLobW3..

49 BrainyQuote, https://www.brainyquote.com/quotes/connie_stevens_
    197013.

50 https://twitter.com/foundmyfitness/status/1430938112369197061?lang=en.

51 Good Reads, https://www.goodreads.com/
    quotes/8094-there-must-be-quite-a-few-things-that-a-hot.

52 Michael Gach, Acupressure's Potent Points, (New York: Bantam, 2011).

53 Rory Vaden, Take the Stairs, (New York: Penguin, 2012).

54 Dr. Kimberly VanBuren, "Start the Reset Program," Balancing Act, https://
    www.balancingactlms.com/start-the-reset.

55 Matthew Walker, Why We Sleep.

56 "Binaural Beats: Sleep, Therapy, and Meditation," Healthline Media,
    November 5, 2021, https://www.healthline.com/health/binaural-beats.

57 Shawn Stevenson, Sleep Smarter, (Emmaus: Rodale, 2016).

58 Daniel Noyed, "Weighted Blanket Research Methodology," Sleep Foundation,
    March 11, 2022, https://www.sleepfoundation.org/research-methodology/
    weighted-blanket.

59 "What's the Best Temperature for Sleep?" Cleveland Clinic, November 16,
    2021, https://health.clevelandclinic.org/what-is-the-ideal-sleeping
    -temperature-for-my-bedroom/.

60 Rob Newsom, "How Blue Light Affects Sleep," Sleep Foundation, October
    18, 2022, https://www.sleepfoundation.org/bedroom-environment/blue-
    light#:~:text=Blue%20light%20suppresses%20the%20body's,we're%20
    trying%20to%20sleep.

61 Kelly Murray, "I Wear My Blue Blockers at Night," https://
    kellymurrayadultsleep.com/articles/i-wear-my-sunglasses-at-night.

62 Tony Robbins, Life Force, (New York: Simon and Schuster, 2022).

63 Aubrey Marcus, Own the Day, Own Your Life.

64 Elizabeth Elkin, "Anthony Bourdain's 10 Most Inspirational Quotes,"
    CNN, June 8, 2020, https://www.cnn.com/ampstories/us/anthony-
    bourdains-10-most-inspirational-quotes.

65 Quote Fancy, https://quotefancy.com/quote/1375496/Questlove-The-only
    -mofos-in-my-circle-are-people-that-I-can-learn-from.

66 Good Reads, https://www.goodreads.com/
    quotes/4473069-a-mentor-is-someone-who-sees-more-talent-and-ability.

67 Maxime Lagacé, "How To Be Happy: The 6 Happiness Pillars You Must
    Know," Wisdom Quotes, https://wisdomquotes.com/how-to-be-happy/.

68 Ramit Sethi, I Will Teach You To Be Rich, (New York: Workman Publishing
    Company, 2009).

69 Dave Ramsey, The Total Money Makeover, (Nashville: Thomas Nelson, 2013).

70 Alisa Wolfson, "Warren Buffett Says This Is the 'Biggest Mistake' People Make With Their Money (and Psst: It Has to Do With Savings)," MarketWatch, August 13, 2022, https://www.marketwatch.com/picks/ warren-buffett-says-this-is-the-biggest-mistake-people-make-with-their- money-and-psst-it-has-to-do-with-savings-01659574976.

71 Morgan Housel, The Psychology of Money, (Petersfield: Harriman House Limited, 2020).

72 Peter Drucker, Managing Oneself, (Boston: Harvard Business Press, 2008).

73 Goodreads, https://www.goodreads.com/author/quotes/13767119. Cornelius_J_.

74 David Schwartz, The Magic of Thinking Big, (New York: Simon and Schuster, 2015).

75 Tony Robbins, MONEY Master the Game, (New York: Simon and Schuster, 2016).

76 Richard Koch, The 80/20 Principle, Expanded and Updated, (New York: Broadway Business, 1999).

77 Greg McKeown, Essentialism, (London: Virgin Books, 2021).

78 Definition of Parkinson's Law, Atlassian, https://www.atlassian.com/blog/ productivity/what-is-parkinsons-law.

79 Mike Michalowicz, Profit First, (New York: Portfolio, reissue edition 2017).

80 Edward De Bono, Six Thinking Hats, (London: Penguin UK, 2016).

81 Jack Flynn, "20 Vital Smartphone Usage Statistics [2023]: Facts, Data, and Trends on Mobile Use in the US," Zippia, October 20, 2022, https://www. zippia.com/advice/smartphone-usage-statistics/.

82 "#648: James Clear, Atomic Habits—Simple Strategies for Building (and Breaking) Habits, Questions for Personal Mastery and Growth, Tactics for Writing and Launching a Mega-Bestseller, Finding Leverage, and More, The Tim Ferriss Show, Apple Podcasts, https://podcasts.apple.com/us/podcast/ 648-james-clear-atomic-habits-simple-strategies-for/id863897795?i= 1000592431628.

83 Nir Eyal, Indistractable, (New York: Bloomsbury Publishing, 2020).

84 James Clear, Atomic Habits, New York: Penguin, 2018.

85 Greg McKeown, Essentialism.

86 Brian Tracy, Eat That Frog! (National Geographic Books, 2017).

87 Hal Elrod, The Miracle Morning, (London: John Murray, 2012).

88 Jim Miller, Budgeting Doesn't Have to Suck, (RMWP, 2020).

89 Jim Kwik, Limitless, (Carlsbad: Hay House, 2020).

90 Chris Guillebeau, The $100 Startup, (New York: Crown, 2012).

91 "Americans Spend 293 Hours Driving Each Year," Automotive Fleet, September 8, 2016, https://www.automotive-fleet.com/136735/americans-spend-an-average-of-17-600-minutes-driving-annually.

92 BrainyQuote, https://www.brainyquote.com/quotes/les_brown_387329.

93 Good Reads, https://www.goodreads.com/quotes/910217-absorb-what-is-useful-discard-what-is-useless-and-add.

94 Alex Banayan, The Third Door, (Sydney: Currency, 2018).

95 Bob Burg and John David Mann, The Go-Giver, (New York: Penguin, 2015).

96 "A Great Teammate Is a Great Listener," NYTimes, February 15, 2014, https://www.nytimes.com/2014/02/16/business/a-great-teammate-is-a-great-listener.html.

97 Brené Brown, Daring Greatly, (New York: Penguin, 2015).

98 Good Reads, https://www.goodreads.com/quotes/23088-if-you-have-an-apple-and-i-have-an-apple.

99 Kevin Horsley, Unlimited Memory, (At Real Estate Solutions LLC, 2021).

100 Jocko Willink, Extreme Ownership, (New York: St. Martin's Press, 2017).

101 James Altucher, Choose Yourself!, (Scotts Valley: CreateSpace Independent Publishing Platform, 2013).

102 Charlie Jones, Life Is Tremendous, (Carol Stream: Tyndale Momentum, 1981).

103 Dave Ramsey, The Total Money Makeover.

104 Stephen Covey, The 7 Habits of Highly Effective People, (London: Simon & Schuster, 2013).

105 George Clason, The Richest Man in Babylon, (Scotts Valley: CreateSpace Independent Publishing Platform, 2015).

106 Denzel Washington, "The Mentors He'll Never Forget." Guideposts, January 1, 2007, https://guideposts.org/positive-living/the-mentors-hell-never-forget/.

107 Robert Kiyosaki, Rich Dad Poor Dad, (Lulu Press, Inc, 2016.)

108 Gaur Gopal Das, Life's Amazing Secrets, (Gurgaon: Penguin Ananda, 2018).

109 Blaise Pascal, Pensées, (London: Penguin Classics, 1995).

110 Timothy Ferriss, The 4-Hour Workweek.

111 Roy T. Bennett, The Light in the Heart.

112 Robin Sharma, The Monk Who Sold His Ferrari, (San Francisco: HarperCollins, 1999).

113 Jairek Robbins, Live It!, (Grand Harbor Press, 2014).

114 Adrienne Bankert, Your Hidden Superpower, (New York: HarperCollins Leadership, 2020).

115 "The Secret to Happiness?" Harvard Health Publishing, October 5, 2017, https://www.health.harvard.edu/blog/the-secret-to-happiness-heres-some-advice-from-the-longest-running-study-on-happiness-2017100512543.

116 Navalism, Twitter, https://twitter.com/NavalismHQ/status/1505914323188731910.

117 David Goggins, Can't Hurt Me, (David Goggins, 2021).

118 Evan Carmichael, Built to Serve, (Houston: Savio Republic, 2020).

119 Bill Perkins, Die with Zero, (Boston: Mariner Books, reprint edition, 2021).

120 Timothy Ferriss, The 4-Hour Workweek.

121 Rolf Potts, Vagabonding, (New York: Ballantine Books, 2002).

122 Rolf Potts, Souvenir, (New York: Bloomsbury Publishing, 2018).

123 Miguel Ruiz, The Mastery of Self, (San Antonio: Hierophant Publishing, 2017).

124 Marianne, Williamson, A Return to Love, (New York: HarperCollins, 2009).

125 Eric Jorgenson, The Almanack of Naval Ravikant, (New Delhi: HarperCollins, 2021).

126 James Allen, As a Man Thinketh, (Scotts Valley: CreateSpace Independent Publishing Platform, 2014).

127 Good Reads, https://www.goodreads.com/quotes/209560-we-must-all-suffer-from-one-of-two-pains-the.

128 Ray Dalio, Principles, (London: Simon & Schuster, 2018).

129 Will Bowen, A Complaint Free World. (New York: Harmony Books, 2013).

130 "20 Inspirational Quotes About Patience," Yahoo Finance, April 22, 2020, https://finance.yahoo.com/photos/20-inspiratoinalquotes-patience-204700533/.

131 BrainyQuote, https://www.brainyquote.com/quotes/voltaire_100338.

132 Quote Fancy, https://quotefancy.com/quote/803281/Ernest-Hemingway-Listen-now-When-people-talk-listen-completely-Don-t-be-thinking-what-you.

133 Good Reads, https://www.goodreads.com/quotes/7887-and-those-who-were-seen-dancing-were-thought-to-be.

134 Go Lean Six Sigma, https://goleansixsigma.com/the-best-time-to-plant-a-tree-was-20-years-ago-the-second-best-time-is-now-chinese-proverb/.

135 Maya Angelou, I Know Why the Caged Bird Sings, (New York: Random House, 2010).

136 Vanessa Van Edwards, Cues, (London: Penguin Business, 2022).

137 Merriam-Webster Dictionary, s.v. "memento mori."

138 Seneca, On the Shortness of Life.

139 Philip Gabbard, Personal Communication, 2022.

140 Marie Kondo, The Life-Changing Magic of Tidying Up, (New York: Random House, 2015).

141 Leo Buscaglia, Living, Loving & Learning, (New York: Ballantine Books, 1985).

142 Timothy Ferriss, The 4-Hour Workweek.

143 Oprah Winfrey, Who Mentored You, January 22, 2015, https://www.hsph. harvard.edu/wmy/celebrities/oprah-winfrey/.

144 Marcus Aurelius, Meditations, (London: Penguin Classics, 2006).

THIS BOOK WAS PUBLISHED IN PARTNERSHIP WITH

booklaunchers

Write, publish, and promote your own brand and business-building bestseller with the help of the Book Launchers team.

Guided by their team of publishing professionals, you'll get:

- ☑ Their #noboringbooks process to write a book that is set up to sell with your specific goals in mind.

- ☑ Marketing layered into every step as they help you write, edit, design, publish, and then promote your non-fiction book.

- ☑ Full control of your book, including all rights and royalties.

Contact Book Launchers and mention Nick's name to receive a free month of post-launch marketing with your membership to their service.

Visit **booklaunchers.com**
to schedule your book positioning call today!

Book Launchers is your professional self-publishing partner.
Learn more tips and insights at: www.booklaunchers.tv

Printed in the USA
CPSIA information can be obtained
at www.ICGtesting.com
LVHW012246211023
761650LV00019B/631